Twayne's English Authors Series

Sylvia E. Bowman, *Editor*

INDIANA UNIVERSITY

Robert Fergusson

24

Robert Fergusson

By ALLAN H. MacLAINE
University of Rhode Island

Twayne Publishers, Inc. :: New York

Library of Congress Catalog Card Number: 65-18225

TO MY FATHER,
ALLAN MACLAINE,
who first aroused
my interest in the
poetry of Scotland

MANUFACTURED IN THE UNITED STATES OF AMERICA

Contents

Preface

Chronology

1. Fergusson and the Tradition 15

2. Apprentice Work (1765-1771) and Later Poems in English 22

3. First Fame: Scots Poems of 1772 32

4. Scots Poems of 1773: "Caller Water" to "Leith Races" 74

5. Scots Poems of 1773: "Ode to the Gowdspink" to "Auld Reikie" 113

6. Fergusson and Burns: Conclusion 152

Notes and References 165

Selected Bibliography 170

Index 174

Preface

The poetry of Scotland comprises a long, rich, distinguished tradition. Yet this poetic heritage, apart from Burns, has received little attention from students of British literature; it remains almost virgin territory. For this state of affairs at least three certain reasons may be adduced. First, the language barrier, though surmountable with moderate effort, remains an obstacle for modern readers. Second, though Scots poetry shows in every period important connections with the English tradition, it represents to a considerable degree an independent development. Consequently, most students of English literature touch upon the Scots at two points only: they hear vaguely of the so-called "Scottish Chaucerians" of the fifteenth century, and they meet Robert Burns in the late eighteenth; the rest is ignored. Finally, the towering figure of Burns has tended to overshadow everything else, so that for most readers Scots poetry *is* Burns and nothing more. And thus it happens that for even so remarkable and exciting a poet as Robert Fergusson this book represents the first, full critical study.

Though Fergusson has never ceased to be read—over forty separate editions of his poems have appeared since his death—he has suffered comparative neglect at the hands of literary historians and critics who have usually dismissed him with brief, uncritical appraisals. In our own day, however, a dramatic reassessment of Fergusson seems to be in the making. This trend is evident in the recent editions of 1947, 1948, and 1956, and, more especially, in the fresh commentaries on Fergusson's poetic quality and stature by such critics as John Speirs, David Daiches, Sydney Goodsir Smith, Matthew P. McDiarmid, and Kurt Wittig. McDiarmid's splendid edition (Volume I: biography and criticism; Volume II: poems and notes) is easily the most impressive piece of Fergusson scholarship yet to appear. After nearly two centuries, the Edinburgh poet seems at last to be coming into his own.

These recent contributions to our understanding of Fergusson, however, though excellent, leave something to be desired on the critical side; they tend to be either generalized views of Fergusson's overall achievement in its historical setting, or separate studies of special aspects of his work. A thorough-going and detailed critical examination of all the significant poetry has yet to appear. The present study is an attempt to fill that gap and to obtain, through a careful analysis of the major poems as works of art, a more precise definition of Fergusson's distinctive quality as a poet than has hitherto been available. To demonstrate the amazingly rapid and fascinating development of Fergusson's powers, I have arranged the material for the most part in chronological order. In this way I hope to do critical justice, long overdue, to one of the most extraordinary of Scots poets.

My large indebtedness to many commentators on Fergusson from the time of Alexander Grosart to the present is, I hope, adequately acknowledged in the notes. To several individuals, however, I owe a special word of thanks. For helpful and constructive critical readings of the manuscript at various stages I am most grateful to Professor I. J. Kapstein of Brown University; to the distinguished Scots poet and champion of Fergusson, Mr. Sydney Goodsir Smith of Edinburgh; and to that keen and knowledgeable devotee of Scots literature, Mr. Robin Lorimer of Edinburgh. Dr. G. Ross Roy of Texas Technological College, editor of *Studies in Scottish Literature,* has generously given me permission to reprint from that journal certain parts of two essays —"Robert Fergusson's *Auld Reikie* and the Poetry of City Life" (*SSL,* Vol. I), and "The *Christis Kirk* Tradition: Its Evolution in Scots Poetry to Burns" (*SSL,* Vol. II). I wish also to thank the Research Committee of Texas Christian University for a grant which paid for the expert typing of the manuscript by Mrs. Aubyn Kendall of Fort Worth. Finally, I owe the greatest debt of all to my wife Sara, herself an enthusiastic Fergussonian, who has patiently read and reread the manuscript and has contributed in countless ways to whatever merit the work may have.

North Providence, R. I. ALLAN H. MACLAINE

Chronology

1750 Robert Fergusson born September 5 in Cap-and-Feather Close, Edinburgh, second son of William Fergusson, clerk, and Elizabeth Forbes, both originally from Aberdeenshire.

1757 Attended Mr. Philp's private school in Niddry's Wynd, Edinburgh.

1758-1762 A student at the High School of Edinburgh, though suffering from intermittent ill health.

1762-1764 Attended the Grammar School of Dundee, having been awarded a David Fergusson bursary which also provided for a subsequent four years at St. Andrews.

1764 Accompanied his mother in August on visit with prosperous uncle John Forbes of Roundlichnot, near old Meldrum, Aberdeenshire. Entered the University of St. Andrews on December 9.

1764-1768 At St. Andrews. First experiments in verse, including the brilliant satire "Elegy on the Death of Mr. David Gregory." Friendship with professor-poet William Wilkie. Father died in May, 1767, leaving family very poor.

1768 Left St. Andrews in May; returned to Edinburgh seeking work to support mother and sister.

1769 Six-month visit with John Forbes of Roundlichnot, who was expected to find him a suitable position, ended in failure. Secured work in September as copyist of legal documents in Commissary Office, Edinburgh, the only regular position he ever held.

1770 Continued production of insipid English verses—pastorals, elegies, burlesques—modeled chiefly on Shenstone.

1771 Began connection with Ruddiman's *Weekly Magazine*, February 7, with publication therein of three "Pastorals." During the year he contributed eight imitative English poems to this journal.

1772 Publication in the *The Weekly Magazine,* January 2, of his first published Scots poem "The Daft-Days," the first of a brilliant series of nine printed in this year. During the same period seventeen trite English poems also appeared in the magazine. Admitted to membership in the Cape Club of Edinburgh on October 10.

1773 Publication of a slim collected volume of *Poems* by Robert Fergusson, including nine in Scots, in January. Later in the same year appeared *Auld Reikie, A Poem* in separate pamphlet, and sixteen other Scots poems in the *The Weekly Magazine,* together with twelve in English. Very active in Cape Club. Spent month of August in country at North Belton, near Dunbar. Visited Dumfries in September. Beginning of serious illness in October which forced him to give up his work at Commissary Office by end of the year. This year was by far his finest and most prolific period as a poet.

1774 Seriously ill and depressed from January to May, but with temporary recovery in June and July. In late July a fall on a staircase caused relapse and intermittent insanity. Committed to Edinburgh madhouse in August. Died October 17 at twenty-four; buried in Canongate Churchyard.

Robert Fergusson

CHAPTER 1

Fergusson and the Tradition

To the Hon[ble] the Bailies of the Canongate, Edinburgh
Gentlemen,

I am sorry to be told that the remains of Robert Fergusson, the so justly celebrated Poet, a man whose talents, for ages to come, will do honor to our Caledonian name, lie in your church-yard, among the ignoble Dead, unnoticed and unknown. . . .

I petition you then, Gentlemen, for your permission to lay a simple stone over his revered ashes, to remain an unalienable property to his deathless fame.–

I have the honor to be, Gentlemen,
your very humble servant
Robert Burns[1]

Edin[r] 6th Feb.
1787

IN this formal but strangely touching letter, Scotland's greatest poet records his protest against the unfeeling neglect of talent and speaks out for the dignity of art. What he says serves to emphasize two facts: the undeserved obscurity in which Robert Fergusson's name lingered, and the overwhelming sense of gratitude which Burns felt towards him. Just over twelve years before this letter was written, Fergusson had died in an Edinburgh madhouse at the age of twenty-four, after a few brief but brilliant and prolific years of poetic activity. And Burns never tired of acknowledging his debt to the Edinburgh poet whom he called "my elder brother in misfortune, / By far my elder brother in the Muse."[2] This fulsome and often repeated praise of Fergusson has usually been dismissed as grossly exaggerated (Burnsian hyperbole), but Burns knew better than anyone else that his "discovery" of Fergusson had been the turning point in his career, that in Fergusson he had finally found himself. Moreover, recent studies have made it increasingly clear that Fergusson was not only the one really decisive influence upon Burns, but also, in his own right, one of the most significant figures in the history of Scots poetry. A brief glance at the Scots tradition which produced him will help to place Fergusson in this perspective.

I *The Scots Poetic Tradition*

When Robert Fergusson burst upon the literary scene of Scotland in the 1770's, the native poetic tradition was in a rather precarious state. In the early part of the century, a group of writers and editors, led by Allan Ramsay, had attempted with partial success to revive interest in the ancient and honorable Scots literary tradition, and to bridge an almost fatal gap in the development of a distinctive national literature. This gap, separating medieval from modern Scots literature, resulted from the long barren period of about 1570 to 1700, during which time the strong and bright current of poetic writing in Scots had been reduced to an intermittent trickle. So long and severe had been the blight upon Scots literature that, by the opening of the eighteenth century, the very names of the great makers of the medieval past—William Dunbar, Robert Henryson, King James I—were half forgotten, while many of their works survived only in obscure and scattered manuscripts. It was as though Scotland had chosen not to remember that she had once had a proud and distinguished literature.

In the fifteenth and early sixteenth centuries, the "golden age" of the old tradition, the situation had been very different indeed. Then the Scottish court had been the center for a brilliant, versatile national literature held in high esteem throughout Europe, and far surpassing in artistic quality the work produced in England during the same period. The Scots poetry of this fruitful age can be divided into three broad classifications. First, there was the sophisticated courtly poetry with its "termes aureate," its dream-visions, love lyrics, and elaborate moral allegories. This poetry was essentially medieval and international in character, though expressed in a distinctively Scots literary language. In the fifteenth century this "aureate" tradition is represented by such poems as "The Kingis Quair" of James I, "The Testament of Cresseid" of Henryson, and "The Goldyn Targe" of Dunbar, and in the sixteenth century by the graceful lyrics of Alexander Scott, "The Cherrie and the Slae" of Alexander

Montgomerie, and the courtly poems of Sir David Lindsay and Sir Richard Maitland. Second, at the other end of the scale, there was the folk poetry, consisting of popular ballads and songs of the common people. Finally, there was a third and very important type of poetry: the artistic treatment of folk themes. Into this broad category fall such poems as the fifteenth-century "Christis Kirk on the Green" and "Peblis to the Play" (attributed to James I); Henryson's "Fables"; Scott's "Justing and Debait"; much of the best work of Dunbar, Lindsay, and Maitland; and a great bulk of poems by unknown authors.

What happened in Scotland to account for the sudden withering of this vigorous poetic tradition toward the close of the sixteenth century? Among many possible causes, three may be adduced as certain. One was the triumph of Knoxian Calvinism, which proscribed poetry along with other "lewd" entertainments and brought such powerful social and moral pressure to bear that it succeeded in virtually stifling poetic creation in Scotland except among a handful of the aristocracy. A second severe blow was the removal in 1603 of the court, which had always been the center of poetic patronage, from Edinburgh to London. Finally, the overwhelming influence of the great English poetry of the late sixteenth and seventeenth centuries persuaded the few Scottish gentlemen who (like Drummond of Hawthornden) continued to practice the art to turn their backs upon the old native tradition and to follow the Elizabethan English style. The result was an almost complete break in the development of sophisticated poetry in the Scots tongue, though the folk poetry did continue to thrive obscurely in oral transmission through the long winter of the seventeenth century despite the Kirk's disapproval. From the whole seventeenth century only a handful of new art poems in Scots have come down to us, written by country gentlemen of the type of Drummond or the Sempills of Beltrees. Among these sporadic efforts "The Life and Death of Habbie Simson" (ca. 1640) by Robert Sempill of Beltrees should be mentioned as the prototype of the comic-elegy genre which became immensely popular in the next century. But, generally speaking, the seventeenth century is a dismal and almost fatal hiatus in the history of Scots poetry.

The revival of interest in the native poetic tradition, which took place in the early decades of the eighteenth century, came in the wake of a renewed sense of Scottish nationalism. The parliamentary Union of 1707, which reduced Scotland politically to the status of a British province, provoked a profound cultural reaction. Many Scots, suffering from a feeling of injured dignity and political betrayal, were stirred to reassert their country's ancient cultural identity and to resist assimilation by England. The result was an extraordinary cultural resurgence, which produced an imposing array of internationally famous philosophers, physicians, architects, lawyers, historians, and men of letters; and this renaissance turned Edinburgh into "the Athens of the North," one of the most dynamic intellectual centers in Europe. In literature, some (like Thomson and Boswell) tried to outdo the English in their own literary idiom; others (like Ramsay and his followers) attempted to reinvigorate the native poetic language and tradition.

The Scots poetic revival in the eighteenth century, then, was essentially a nationalistic movement, the effort of some sections of a small and economically poor nation to reaffirm its cultural integrity. It was heralded by the publication of James Watson's epoch-making anthology, *A Choice Collection of Comic and Serious Scots Poems, both Antient and Modern* (Edinburgh, 1706, 1709, 1711), and pioneered by the versatile Allan Ramsay. Ramsay's work as an editor and publicist of Scots poetry (*The Ever Green*, 1724; *The Tea-Table Miscellany*, 1724) met with instantaneous success; moreover, his original poetry in the vernacular—though by no means first-rate—restored to vigorous life several traditional Scots genres. In the latter respect, however, Ramsay's achievement was limited. The Scots tongue had been so long in disuse as a vehicle for serious poetry that Ramsay felt able to use it, for the most part, only for comic verse and songs; in his serious poetry, Ramsay usually reverted to labored neo-Classical English. Even so, Ramsay's many-faceted and untiring effort as a restorer of literary Scots was of great historical importance and formed an indispensable foundation for the later work of Fergusson and Burns.

The personal influence and example of Allan Ramsay stimulated several younger writers to follow his lead; but, during the long period from about 1730 to 1770 (Ramsay himself virtually stopped writing in 1728), no Scots poet of comparable stature appeared. As a result, the vernacular revival, so auspiciously launched in the first quarter of the century, seemed to be in serious danger of petering out altogether for lack of adequate leadership. This danger, however, was fortunately averted by the sudden emergence in 1772 of a compelling new voice in Scots poetry—that of an obscure Edinburgh legal clerk, Robert Fergusson.

II *Fergusson's Career*

Fergusson was born in Cap-and-Feather Close, Edinburgh, on September 5, 1750, of a respectable lower middle-class family. Both of his parents were from Aberdeenshire where his father, William Fergusson, had been clerk to an Aberdeen merchant. Shortly before the poet's birth, the family had moved to Edinburgh where his father secured a series of poorly paid clerical positions until his premature death in 1767. Thus, Fergusson was born and nurtured in the very heart of "Auld Reekie," the grimy, incredibly crowded, yet strangely beautiful old city of Edinburgh —a city which he grew to love with a profound and touching affection and which he re-created graphically in his poetry.

Though the Fergussons were wretchedly poor, they did their best to give their four children good educations. Robert, after some private schooling, was sent to the High School of Edinburgh for the full term of four years (1758-1762). He did well enough there to be awarded a special bursary, which provided full maintenance for two more years of study at the Grammar School of Dundee, and subsequently, if found qualified, for four years at the University of St. Andrews. Thanks to this generous bursary, Fergusson was able to go to St. Andrews, where he was admitted to St. Salvator College in December, 1764.

Fergusson's four years at St. Andrews (1764-1768), despite niggardly rations and miserable accommodations, were probably the happiest in his brief career. He soon earned a reputation as a light-hearted prankster and as a writer of witty verse-satires on the professors, one of which, the daring and promising "Elegy on the Death of Mr. David Gregory," has survived. At the same time, he got a sound Classical education, won the firm friendship of the eccentric Professor William Wilkie, and did extensive reading in poetry—Latin, English, and Scots.

When Fergusson finished his fourth year at St. Andrews in 1768, his formal education necessarily came to an end. His father had died in May, 1767, and it became imperative for Fergusson to support his widowed mother. Further professional training in the law or in the ministry, which he may have contemplated, was now out of the question. After a fruitless trip to Aberdeenshire, where he had hoped to get a start in life through the good offices of his prosperous uncle, John Forbes of Roundlichnot, Fergusson returned in despair to Edinburgh. For a few months he did clerical odd jobs until he finally secured a permanent position—the only one he was ever to hold—as a copyist of legal documents for Charles Abercrombie, who was deputy clerk of the Commissary Office, a government legal department. Thus, by September, 1769, Fergusson got his start in one of the most drudging and utterly dispiriting occupations imaginable—the endless copying of endless documents.

Soon after his settlement in Edinburgh, Fergusson resumed his experimental writing of verses and seems quickly to have acquired a local reputation as a poet. By the spring of 1771 he had become a regular contributor to a popular journal, *The Weekly Magazine, or Edinburgh Amusement,* published by Walter and Thomas Ruddiman. In that year, eight of his poems in hackneyed neo-Classical English appeared in the magazine, most of them worthless imitations of Shenstone. It would be hard to imagine a less promising beginning in poetry. Quite suddenly, however, in January, 1772, he reverted to the native poetic tradition with "The Daft-Days," the first of a series of thirty-one brilliant Scots poems which flowed from his pen with ever-increasing and astonishing frequency through the following two years. These poems brought Fergusson almost immediate national fame, but no substantial patronage; he was forced to stick at his dreary job in the Commissary Office. But by the fall of 1772, letters were pouring in from delighted readers all over Scotland, acclaiming him as a new national poet and the legitimate successor to Ramsay ("Is Allan risen frae the deid?"). Two immediate results were Fergusson's election to the distinguished Cape Club of Edinburgh in October, 1772, and the publication of a slim volume of his *Poems* in the next year. Almost overnight the impoverished young legal clerk had become an Edinburgh celebrity.

But Fergusson's triumph was short-lived. His health had never been good; toward the end of 1773 it was strained beyond the breaking point by overwork (he was writing at a feverish pace) and by his strenuous social life. In January, 1774, he collapsed with a severe physical and nervous disorder.[3] After several months of fluctuating illness, the final blow came in late July when, feeling somewhat better, Fergusson went out to visit a friend and fell down a flight of stone stairs. He suffered a concussion and some brain injury which resulted in violent, intermittent insanity. His distracted mother was forced to commit him to the Edinburgh madhouse for paupers, a grim old building called "the Schelles" or "Cells," where on October 17, 1774,[4] just a few weeks after his twenty-fourth birthday, Robert Fergusson died in the night.

The tragic brevity of Fergusson's career—he did all of his best work in two short years—has tended to obscure the true nature of his achievement. Eclipsed as he was almost immediately by Burns, Fergusson has usually been relegated by historians of literature to the anomalous position of a "forerunner"; seldom has he been treated as a poet in his own right. This approach has encouraged the view of Fergusson as a boy-poet with a lucky gift, who dashed off a few vivid sketches of Edinburgh life and then died and whose only importance is that he happened to have stimulated Burns. But Burns knew better; his poetic instinct recognized the astonishing power and maturity of Fergusson's work which he valued above Ramsay's as, up to his own time, the finest Scots poetry of the century. And Burns was right.

CHAPTER 2

Apprentice Work (1765-1771) and Later Poems in English

THE works of Robert Fergusson perfectly illustrate the strange dualism in eighteenth-century Scottish poetry: the attempt to write in both the home-bred Scottish manner and in the genteel neo-Classical English style. In no other Scottish poet of the century, including Burns himself, is the contrast between Scottish and English work so pronounced and striking as it is in Fergusson. His vernacular poems are usually fresh, original, and brilliantly executed; his poems in English, with few exceptions, are imitative, trite, and worthless as literature. There is, in fact, a curious parallelism between the poetic apprenticeship of Fergusson and that of Burns. Apart from occasional and tentative experiments with Scots song, the early career of Burns as a poet is largely a story of misguided talent, of futile efforts to beat the English at their own game. Burns wasted long years trying to imitate one English poet after another—Pope, Gray, Thomson, the "divine Shenstone"—and generally failed miserably. Fergusson was fortunate enough to find himself earlier than Burns, but the pattern of their apprentice work is very much the same.

Fergusson began as a student at St. Andrews (1764-1768) with two vigorous Scots poems which showed promise. Then, with his return to Edinburgh in 1768, he abruptly abandoned his native tongue and (probably seduced by the desire of capturing an aristocratic audience) switched to the genteel tradition, turning out a long series of lifeless poetical essays in neo-Classical English. Finally, and just as abruptly, he returned to the vernacular and achieved his first real success in "The Daft-Days" (January, 1772).

"The Daft-Days" is the first of ten brilliant Scots poems which Fergusson produced in 1772, and marks the beginning of his discovery of himself, of the peculiar bent of his genius. Though he continued to write English poems through 1772 (and, in fact, throughout his brief career), his interest in the native poetic tradition became increasingly dominant during this crucial year, culminating in the ambitious and sparkling "Hallow-fair" (November, 1772). Like Burns, Fergusson was at first misled by an adolescent desire to be fashionable; he had, therefore, to experience a groping and frustrating apprenticeship before he could discover the kind of poetry in which he could excel. But once he sensed the secret of his own precocious and extraordinary powers, Fergusson's genius developed with astonishing rapidity. By the fall of 1772 he was ready to produce his finest work.

I *First Experiments in Scots Verse*

As we have seen, Fergusson began as a poet with two experiments in "plain braid Scots." Perhaps the earliest of his surviving works is a fourteen-line translation of "Horace, Ode 11, Lib. I" into Scots tetrameter couplets, which was first printed in Ruddiman's 1779 edition of Fergusson among "Posthumous Pieces." Its immaturity suggests an early date; it is most probably a product of Fergusson's student years at St. Andrews.[1] At any rate, Fergusson's paraphrase is clearly derivative. Most of the Scottish poets of his century shared a fondness for Horace, and more especially for the Horatian ideal of a quiet life of literary leisure. They never tired of translating and imitating the odes and epistles of the graceful Latin poet. Indeed, several other translations of this very ode of Horace appeared in Scotland during the eighteenth century, including a verbose English version by William Hamilton of Bangour, and one in Scots by Allan Ramsay.[2] Ramsay's brief but spirited rendition in the sixth and seventh stanzas of his "Third Epistle to William Hamilton of Gilbertfield" seems to have been the immediate inspiration for Fergusson's little poem, the whole of which is given here (italics are Fergusson's in all quotations):

Ne'er fash your *thumb* what *gods* decree	bother yourself
To be the *weird* o' you or me,	fate
Nor deal in *cantrup's* kittle cunning	magic's difficult

To speir how fast your days are running,	ask
But patient lippen for the *best,*	hope
Nor be in *dowy thought* opprest,	sad
Whether we see mare winters come	more
Than this that spits wi' canker'd foam.	
Now moisten weel your *geyzen'd wa'as*	dried out walls
Wi' couthy friends and *hearty blaws;*	sociable; drinks
Ne'er lat your *hope* o'ergang your *days,*	outstrip
For *eild* and *thraldom* never stays;	old age
The day looks *gash,* toot aff your *horn,*	fair; drink
Nor care yae *strae* about the *morn.*	a straw*

Fergusson's heavy debt to Ramsay here—obvious in his use of "Ne'er fash," "cantrup's," and the "horn . . . morn" rime—is evidence that he was reading Ramsay at a very early age.

The poem is, however, significant in itself. Although it is no more than a poetical exercise, yet, judged as the work of a lad of fourteen or fifteen and as an example of Fergusson's apprentice hand, it is remarkably well executed. The "Horace" reveals Fergusson's sensitive feeling for words, already apparent here. For example, the poem opens breezily with the colloquial expression "Ne'er fash your thumb." Fergusson shares with Burns the delightful faculty of turning such racy folk expressions to poetic account. The alliterative phrase, "cantrup's kittle cunning," deftly suggests the devious calculations and ancient mysterious qualities of old-fashioned magic. Here his use of the familiar word, "cantrup," meaning "sorcery," effectively translates Horace's reference to the Roman profession of augury into terms of Scottish folklore. The poem as a whole, slight though it is, gives the first hint of Fergusson's talent for phrase-making, his richly suggestive use of the mother tongue. It reveals, too, something of the verve, the swift movement, and economy of expression which were characteristic of his mature work.

During his first year at college, Fergusson produced a second vernacular poem, the "Elegy on the Death of Mr. David Gregory, Late Professor of Mathematics in the University of St Andrews."

* The marginal gloss, used here and throughout, defines the hard words in each line in their contexts. The reader's common sense will enable him to determine which words or phrases are being defined in each instance. The italics and small capitals in the quotations are Fergusson's, and have no relationship to the gloss.

Professor Gregory died on April 13, 1765; and in view of definite signs of immaturity in the poem, there is no valid reason to doubt, as some of Fergusson's commentators have, that it was written immediately after the event in April, 1765. The elegy no doubt circulated in manuscript among the poet's fellow students at St. Andrews; it never appeared in *The Weekly Magazine,* and was not published until 1773 when Fergusson included it as one of the nine Scottish pieces in his little volume of *Poems.* It remains the best surviving specimen of those verse satires on the professors for which, according to all the biographers, Fergusson was noted at St. Andrews, and his most valuable production before 1772.

Fergusson's "Elegy on Gregory" is a comic elegy in the pure tradition of Robert Sempill's "Life and Death of Habbie Simson" (ca. 1640). Consequently, Fergusson had an abundance of models in earlier Scottish poetry from which to work, and he leaned on them rather heavily. The poem is, indeed, quite imitative, as one might expect in such a youthful effort. It represents Fergusson's earliest known use of the "Habbie" stanza, and his first attempt at the humorous elegy. In its composition he was, significantly, indebted directly and unmistakably to Sempill's "Habbie Simson" itself, the prototype of the genre.[3] The meter, tone, method, and purpose of Fergusson's poem are identical with Sempill's. Like Sempill, Fergusson sets out to praise his subject and make mischievous fun of him at the same time. But the parallelism goes further: Fergusson follows Sempill and his successors (Hamilton of Gilbertfield and Ramsay) in some of his rimes and even in his phraseology. For example, in his opening stanza Fergusson uses the well-worn formula "Without remeid . . . Sin Gregory's dead," which he could have found in Sempill's "Habbie" (stanza 1), Sempill's "Elegy on Sanny Briggs" (stanza 1), or Ramsay's "Elegy on Maggy Johnstoun" (stanza 13). Furthermore, Fergusson's sixth stanza (on football) is very closely modeled on the eighth of Sempill's "Habbie," while the "nap . . . tap" rime in his last stanza was clearly suggested by Ramsay's "I took a Nap . . . As sound's a Tap" ("Maggy Johnstoun," stanza 10).

Other instances of such borrowings from earlier writers might easily be cited, but the above are surely enough to establish the derivative nature of Fergusson's elegy, and to show how stereotyped the "Habbie Simson" genre had become during the hundred years and more which separate Sempill's elegies and Fergusson's "Gregory." The very tightness and narrowness of the tradition, as illustrated in this juvenile poem of Fergusson's, serve to underline the importance of his later work in breaking down the rigid limitations, recurrent rimes, and standardized phrases of the old "Habbie" genre, thereby paving the way for Burns. Finally, Fergusson's indebtedness proves beyond question that at the early age of fourteen he was already deeply immersed in the vernacular poetry of his native land.

The "Elegy on Gregory," judged on its own merits, is an astonishing performance in many ways. Perhaps the most striking thing about it is the extreme daring which Fergusson displayed in writing such a poem. David Gregory was, after all, a real person; yet here is Fergusson, on this sad occasion, writing a comic elegy, full of irreverent joking and good-natured banter at the expense of the deceased. The youngster's audacity must have shocked the more staid members of the faculty and delighted the students. From this point of view Fergusson's elegy is, no doubt, in bad taste; but, since there is absolutely no malice in it, the bad taste is surely excusable in a lad of fourteen. The kind of imaginative daring displayed in this adolescent poem is a characteristic of all Fergusson's Scots poems.

Fergusson gives the poem playful satiric tone by grossly exaggerating the grief of students and faculty and by overpraising Gregory. He reduces Gregory's professional skills to an absurdity, as in this stanza extolling his mathematical abilities:

He could, by *Euclid,* prove lang sine — long ago
A ganging *point* compos'd a line; — moving
By numbers too he cou'd divine,
When he did read,
That *three* times *three* just made up nine;
But now he's dead.
(stanza 3)

The richly comic quality, the "pawky" humor of this stanza, and of the elegy as a whole, are largely achieved through Fergusson's adroit manipulation of the tail-lines to clinch the satiric point of each stanza. The last line of the above stanza, "But now he's dead," for example, coming as it does after a long pause at the end of line 5, and introducing a note of absurdly exaggerated regret, admirably drives home the comic intent of the whole stanza and rounds it off with a laugh. The skill with which this is effected is surely remarkable in so young a poet. Equally notable is the fact that Fergusson never pushes his satiric urge too far; there is no trace of harshness in the poem, no hint of any serious criticism of Gregory. Fergusson pokes impish fun at the dead professor's eccentricities, it is true; but he treats them in a familiar and affectionate spirit, as though Fergusson, despite the sly mockery and high-spirited fun of his poem, really felt a sincere, nostalgic regard for the old professor.

Fergusson's two earliest poems, "Horace" and "Elegy on Gregory," are the best that he was to produce until "The Daft-Days," seven years later. Each is slight in content, immature, and derivative. Their overdependence upon traditional formulas marks them both as experimental exercises. Yet they show astonishing precocity and promise of greater things to come. The technical competence and deftness which they reveal lead us to suspect that they were not, after all, the first of Fergusson's vernacular experiments but the best of several such essays dating from the early St. Andrews period, the only two that Fergusson chose to preserve for publication. However this may be, the poems are extraordinarily good for a boy of fourteen. Imitative though they are in form and subject matter, they have a freshness, a decidedly individual style in language, and a boldness in treatment which stamp them as the work of a solid, original talent.

II *Early Poems in English*

Had Fergusson continued his work along these lines, he might have fulfilled the great promise of his first two attempts at an earlier date and made better use of the short time allotted to him. Unfortunately, however, he abandoned the vernacular and dissipated his poetic energies for the next few years in experiments in the genteel style. Probably his moving from St. Andrews to Edinburgh in 1768-1769 had much to do with this sudden change. At St. Andrews he was writing for fun, entertaining his fellow students with clever little sketches in the mother tongue. The vernacular would do very well at St. Andrews. But in Edinburgh the situation was rather different. There the elegant writings of Pope and Gay, the sentimental poems of Shenstone and Gray were currently the rage, enjoying immense popularity among the literati and gentlefolk of the old northern capital. No doubt Fergusson was ambitious to capture this new high-class audience; and, feeling that he could not hope to do so if he continued his work in the homely native tradition, he transferred his energies and attempted to write in the fashionable English manner.

Of Fergusson's early English poems little need be said. They are all worthless performances, reflecting the worst features of English neo-Classical verse in its decadent period. He seems to have fallen under the spell of Shenstone's sentimental "elegies" and "effusions" in particular, as the following absurd lines from "The Decay of Friendship" (September, 1771) will show:

> When, from the summit of a towering hill,
> My seats of former happiness I spy,
> The tears of sorrow o'er my cheeks distill,
> While mournful thoughts the gushing streams supply.
> (stanza 12)

It seems, indeed, almost incredible that the brilliant young poet of the "Elegy on Gregory" could also have written this insincere, tearful nonsense, or the other driveling "odes," woodenly imitative pastorals, and pedestrian "mock-heroics" that he turned out during these years (1769-1771). These poems are utterly lacking in genuine feeling; most of them, written on themes outside of Fergusson's experience, are filled with trumped up, fashionable emotions which he could not have felt. They must be regarded as misguided attempts to cater to the vitiated tastes of the Edinburgh aristocracy. No significant development of Fergusson's powers is discernible in his English poems of this period. There is a purely mechanical improvement in his handling of English verse forms in the later pieces, it is true, but no real promise of better things to come.

III *Later Poems in English*

Since Fergusson continued writing poems in the southern idiom until the end of his career early in 1774, it is convenient here to say a few words about his later English verse, before coming to a discussion of his far more important and valuable work in Scots.

The strong influence of Shenstone and the eighteenth-century vogue of sentimentality persists in Fergusson's English work well into 1772, as evidenced by such insipid pieces as "Damon to his Friends, A Ballad" (July, 1772), which is modeled on Shenstone's "Pastoral Ballad," and "Against Repining at Fortune" (September, 1772). But toward the end of 1772, the sentimental tendency drops off sharply, and in 1773 Fergusson turned his back on the sentimental tradition altogether, directly attacking it in several places. This complete reversal is the most striking feature of Fergusson's development as a writer of poems in English during this period, and it first reveals itself in "The Sow of Feeling" (April, 1773), the most significant of all Fergusson's English poems.

"The Sow of Feeling" is in its very title a mockery and a repudiation not only of the work of Henry Mackenzie, the "Man of Feeling," but of the whole sentimentalist movement in Scottish literature. Mackenzie was then at the height of his fame, the idol of the Edinburgh literati; for Fergusson to make fun of him in this way must have taken a good deal of courage and self-confidence. The necessary self-confidence, no doubt, came to Fergusson as a result of the success and broad popularity of his Scottish poems. By this time he was securely established as a vernacular poet with a wide popular following, and he probably felt that, since he had failed to excel in the sentimental style anyway, he could now afford to turn his back on the whole sentimental tradition and to concentrate his energies on kinds of poetry more congenial to his mind and temperament.

"The Sow of Feeling" itself, though by no means a brilliant poem, is cleverly conceived and fairly amusing. The poem takes the form of a soliloquy representing the thoughts of a sow whose "husband" and "children" have been taken to the slaughterhouse. She curses the "Malignant planets!" and the "pitiless oppression" of man who has torn from her side her beloved children, "a little suckling race,/ With all their father growing in their face." Then she recalls with tender emotion her husband in his courting days when their love was "a flame divine," when "my trusty lover shook for me/ A show'r of *acorns* from the *oaken* tree."

She describes the "lovely languor of his eye" and the "music of his groans" on the fateful day when he was heartlessly carried off to slaughter. Finally, in accordance with the best sentimental doctrine, the bereaved sow decides to pine away and die of a broken heart, to "resign / Life, to be number'd 'mongst the *feeling swine*." [4]

After the appearance of this poem, the proportion of Fergusson's English poems to his Scottish ones fell off perceptibly, while the English poems which he continued to write were generally satiric and anti-sentimental in tone. In thus decisively repudiating the vogue of sentimentality, Fergusson was daring to swim against the prevailing current in genteel poetry, and in so doing he largely cut himself off from the possibility of patronage. The aristocratic patrons of Edinburgh, and especially the sophisticated literati, would scarcely be anxious to assist a young poet who made fun of their favorite Mackenzie and who dared to scoff at the kind of poetry they worshipped. In this sense, "The Sow of Feeling" marks the turning point in Fergusson's career. From then on, although he continued to make occasional experiments in English satire, such as the sprightly "R. Fergusson's Last Will" and its "Codicil" (which were, ironically enough, the last two of his poems to be published during Fergusson's lifetime), he had virtually committed himself to writing realistic vernacular poetry. He had, in short, found himself. In one decisive stroke he had repudiated all of his previous efforts in the sentimental style.

IV *Turning Point*

After long and apparently exclusive preoccupation with the genteel English tradition through the years 1769 to 1771, Fergusson returned to the vernacular in the last days of 1771 and produced "The Daft-Days," the first of a brilliant series. What made Fergusson turn back so suddenly to his old love of Scots verse? We have no way of knowing for certain, but in all probability he was prompted to do so by a growing sense of his failure in the genteel tradition. By the end of 1771, Fergusson had tried his hand at nearly every type of English neo-Classical verse then fashionable. And he had failed in all of these styles. Being a sensitive and intelligent young man with something of an artistic conscience, Fergusson must have realized that he was on the wrong track altogether. Whether he realized at the same time that his greatest strength lay in the vernacular is doubtful. More likely he reverted to writing in the familiar mother tongue as a further experiment in his long search for an artistic medium. At first, perhaps, he did not even know for sure that he had finally discovered it. But during 1772, as he found himself rapidly achieving fame as a Scots poet, it seems to have slowly dawned on him that his one real opportunity for greatness lay close at home, right under his nose, as it were, in the poetic language and traditions of his native land. He had possessed the secret all the time, if he had only known it; and, had he not been distracted by the desire to be fashionable and been misguided by the praise of his friends, he might have found himself earlier.

CHAPTER 3

First Fame: Scots Poems of 1772

> O for a spunk o' Allan's glee,
> Or Fergusson's, the bauld an' slee . . .
>
> BURNS

I "The Daft-Days"

THROUGHOUT 1771 Walter Ruddiman had been publishing Fergusson's feeble neo-Classical and sentimental imitations in his *Weekly Magazine*. Then suddenly, on Thursday, January 2, 1772, there appeared in the same periodical and over the same signature, "R. Fergusson," a new and startlingly different poem—"The Daft-Days," a delightfully lively description of the Christmas holidays or "daft days" in Auld Reekie (Edinburgh). The poem contrasts sharply with Fergusson's juvenile efforts in the vernacular, the paraphrase of Horace and the "Elegy on Gregory," in being almost entirely original in method, language, and general treatment. In only one stanza, the eighth, does Fergusson seem to be directly indebted to earlier poetry. In it Fergusson probably picked up the idea of resistance to Italian music and encouragement of native musical arts from Ramsay ("Elegy on Patie Birnie," stanzas 6 and 7) and passed it on to Burns ("Cotter's Saturday Night," stanza 13). Fergusson's stanza may also have provided the germinal idea for John Skinner's famous song of "Tullochgorum."

Apart from this single debt to Ramsay, however, "The Daft-Days" is strikingly original and in some ways revolutionary. It is written in the traditional "Habbie" stanza, and represents the first successful attempt in modern Scottish poetry to use the six-line stanza for a poem which is neither a comic elegy nor a poetic epistle. Allan Ramsay in his comic elegies had already hinted at the latent possibilities of the form; but Fergusson, in "The Daft-Days" and in several later poems, was the first to exploit the full potentialities of this stanza as a vehicle for general social description and satire. "The Daft-Days" has, therefore, considerable historical importance, not merely as the first published Scots poem of Fergusson, but as the first decisive step in the further development and extension of the "Habbie" tradition, a development which led directly to Burns's versatile handling of the form and provided him with a brilliant precedent.

"The Daft-Days" is the earliest example of the structural method which was to be strongly characteristic of Fergusson's Scottish poems: it consists of swift-paced description, with frequent and quick transitions, moving briskly from one subject to another, presenting a group of vivid little vignettes one after another, with notable vigor and economy of expression. He usually begins with a general view of the scene, and then goes on to light up specific details within the framework—details carefully selected to build up a vivid and concrete impression of the whole. There is always a danger of looseness and lack of unity inherent in this method, a danger which Fergusson does not always avoid elsewhere. "The Daft-Days," however, is very skillfully constructed: each section leads naturally into the next; all the parts are bound together by the central theme of good cheer and form a harmonious whole.

The poem falls naturally into three major sections, each having its own atmosphere and qualities of style. "The Daft-Days" opens with four introductory stanzas in which Fergusson deftly sets up a contrast, quite common in Scots poetry, between bleak winter weather out of doors and cozy conviviality within. The first stanza, with its richly humorous portrayal of a Scottish winter, has been much admired:

Now mirk December's dowie face — gloomy
Glours our the rigs wi' sour grimace, — over; ridges
While, thro' his *minimum* of space,
The bleer-ey'd sun,
Wi' blinkin light and stealing pace,
His race doth run.

This idea is further developed in the next two stanzas, which, however, are slightly weakened by traces of neo-Classical diction ("od'rous flavour," "*Borean* cave," "visage grave"). But the lively fourth stanza takes us straight to the heart of Fergusson's theme:

Auld Reikie! thou'rt the canty hole,	cheerful
A bield for mony caldrife soul,	shelter; chilly
Wha snugly at thine ingle loll,	fire-place
Baith warm and couth;	sociable
While round they gar the bicker roll	make; wooden vessel
To weet their mouth.	for drinking

This stanza, one of the most perfectly balanced in the poem, rolls sweetly off the tongue when read aloud, filled as it is with Fergusson's touching and profound affection for the grimy old city of his birth. The metaphor, "canty hole," is especially appropriate and rich in suggestiveness, conveying the idea of snug shelter from winter storms and, at the same time, the feeling of deep human happiness and brotherliness in the midst of, and in spite of, the squalid environment of the city itself, the "hole." Here Fergusson completes his outdoor-indoor contrast which makes the perfect introduction to "The Daft-Days." He has brought the reader in out of the storm and has skillfully set the mood of the whole poem: the comfortable feeling of robust human merriment against a background of howling winter blizzards outside.

In the central section of five stanzas, Fergusson re-creates for us the warmth, brightness, and sociability of the "daft days" in Auld Reekie in a series of lively vignettes. The technical brilliance of this part of the poem may be seen in a single illustration of its rhythm. Fergusson here achieves a rising tempo and intensity as he describes in turn the eating, drinking, and dancing joys of the season. Stanza 5, on good things to eat, begins at a moderate pace, then becomes more rapid in stanzas 6 and 7 on drinking, beginning

Ye browster wives, now busk ye bra,	ale-wives; dress finely
And fling your sorrows far awa'.	

Here the movement of the verse is speeded up by the direct exhortation, aided by the explosive value of the alliterative "b's" and "f's". And, after a brief relaxation in stanza 7, the tempo reaches still greater intensity as Fergusson turns to picture the gaiety and abandon of old-fashioned Scottish dances:

Fidlers, your pins in temper fix, — fiddle pegs
And roset weel your fiddle-sticks, — rub with rosin
But banish vile Italian tricks
        From out your quorum,
Nor *fortes* wi' *pianos* mix,
        Gie's *Tulloch Gorum.*

The metrical variation in the first foot of this stanza throws great emphasis on the word "*Fidlers,*" where it naturally belongs; brings out the urgency of the request for music; helps to create the familiar conversational tone and to draw the reader imaginatively into the scene which is laid before him in all its exuberant life and motion. The transition from "Ye browster wives" to "*Fidlers*" is extremely effective in speeding up the rhythm to correspond to the gay, frenzied movement of a Scottish reel. This central section of the poem is executed throughout with remarkable verve and careful craftsmanship.

Fergusson's last two stanzas together form the conclusion of the poem. At stanza 10, the vivid life and motion of his verse are suddenly cut off, and dull generalizing and moralizing creep in as Fergusson switches to standard English. This notorious habit of slipping into self-conscious English to express serious thought was common among Scots poets of Fergusson's century —Burns's "To a Mountain Daisy" and "Cotter's Saturday Night" being, perhaps, the most flagrant examples of it. Here, Fergusson's neo-Classical abstractions and such wooden expressions as, "Let blithesome innocence appear / To crown our joy," make this stanza the weakest in the poem. But the lapse is brief; in the final stanza there is an immediate recovery of shrewd humor, as Fergusson makes a comic prayer to the "great god of *Aqua Vitae,*" who rules Edinburgh, to protect her boisterous citizens from the brutalities of "that black banditti," the City Guard.

The City Guard had long acted as a military police force in Edinburgh, and was mainly recruited from invalid members of Highland regiments. About the middle of the eighteenth century, this Guard seems to have degenerated into a pack of incompetent ruffians who wielded their savage weapons with little sense of either justice or discrimination. As a result, by Fergusson's time they had become objects of ridicule and vilification in the streets of Auld Reekie and were often pelted with mud and refuse by hostile mobs. Fergusson himself seems to have had a special animus against these "black banditti"; he mentions them with scorn in poem after poem, a fact which suggests that he may himself have suffered rough treatment at their hands. Sir Walter Scott, who gives a fascinating and detailed account of the City Guard in *The Heart of Midlothian* (Chapter 3), suggests that the Guard appeared so often in the poems of Fergusson that he might almost "be considered their poet-laureate."

In spite of the tenth stanza, "The Daft-Days" is a delightful and memorable poem. It has wonderful vigor and dash, with, at the same time, a sureness of technique and facile mastery of Scottish idiom which mark it as unquestionably the work of a brilliant and original artist. With "The Daft-Days" Fergusson achieved his first really substantial success as a poet, and seemed finally to have hit upon the type of verse that was to make him famous.

II "Elegy on the Death of Scots Music"

Fergusson's second Scottish poem of 1772, "Elegy on the Death of Scots Music," appeared in Ruddiman's periodical on March 5, three months after "The Daft-Days." Although this poem was written under the general influence of the comic elegy tradition, it is not a comic elegy. It is, in fact, the first example (after Ramsay's rather weak "Ode to the Earl of Hartford" [1728]) in modern Scottish poetry of the use of the six-line stanza in a poem of serious intent, and thus it helped to prepare the way for Burns's use of the stanza as a vehicle for serious thought in such works as "To a Mouse" and "To a Mountain Daisy." That the "Elegy on Scots Music" is, nevertheless, closely related to the comic-elegy tradition is proven by the fact that this poem, like the earlier "Elegy on Gregory," contains traces of the direct influence of Robert Sempill's "Habbie Simson" itself. Fergusson's "dumb-come-hum" (stanza 6) and "reed-dead" (stanza 7) rimes clearly echo the sixth stanza of Sempill's elegy, while, as in

"The Daft-Days," the theme of resistance to Italian music no doubt came from Ramsay's "Patie Birnie." On the other hand, Fergusson's stanza beginning "Mourn ilka nymph and ilka swain, / Ilk sunny hill and dowie glen" may have provided the inspiration for Burn's' "Elegy on Matthew Henderson." [1] Certainly the eighth stanza ("Ilk carline now may grunt and grane," etc.) set the pattern for the opening lines of Burns's "Tam Samson's Elegy" ("Kilmarnock lang may grunt an' grane") and for David Sillar's "Elegy on G. B." ("Auld Irvine now may grunt an' grane").[2]

In its theme, the "Elegy on the Death of Scots Music" is an elaboration of the idea Fergusson had previously touched on briefly in the eighth stanza of his "Daft-Days" ("But banish vile Italian tricks . . . Gie's *Tulloch Gorum*"). He begins with three stanzas recalling the glories of ancient Scots music and mourning its decay; in the central section (stanzas 4-8), he describes the various ways in which life in Scotland has lost zest because of the decline of national music, and laments the passing of one of its most famous exponents, the fiddler Macgibbon; finally (stanzas 9-11), he attacks musical fashions imported from Italy and calls upon all Scots to fight for the restoration of their ancient musical heritage. Each of the eleven stanzas ends with the word "dead"; in fact, the last line of each stanza is in the nature of a refrain which recurs with slight variations, always ending in "dead." This device, which Fergusson inherited from the Sempill tradition, helps to pull the whole poem together and to give it a degree of structural unity.

In style, the "Elegy" is a curious blend of the artificial and the natural. Kurt Wittig, in an interesting discussion of this poem,[3] argues cogently that the stylistic contrast between Classicism and "hameliness" is deliberate on Fergusson's part—a subtly ironic way of underlining the contrast between artificial music from abroad and the home-bred Scottish kind. Wittig also sees the poem as a conscious criticism of the Scoto-English poetic style introduced by Allan Ramsay. A brief look at the text shows how these contrasts are achieved.

Fergusson begins on a moderately artificial, Ramsayesque note:

On Scotia's plains, in days of yore,
When lads and lasses *tartan* wore,
Saft Music rang on ilka shore . . . every

This obviously standard English is seasoned with an occasional Scots word ("ilka") or spelling ("saft"). But in the next three stanzas, Fergusson goes much further by introducing bits of neo-Classical jargon which are wholly inappropriate to his theme. In stanza 2, he has "the feather'd choir," and "the zephyrs of the spring"; in stanza 3, nymphs, swains, "*Naiads*," "weeping streams," and a personified "echo"; and in stanza 4, "the saft vernal breezes." In this first part of the poem, then, we are in the never-never world of neo-Classical pastoralism, with nymphs and "*Naiads*" taken from Greek mythology flourishing "on *Yarrow's* bonny braes." And, if Wittig is right, as I think he is, the effect of stately artificiality is deliberate on Fergusson's part.

Then, in the next two stanzas, the tone suddenly changes as Fergusson abruptly shifts in imagery from the artificial to the real and in style from imported neo-Classical English to native Scots:

Nae lasses now, on simmer days,	summer
Will lilt at bleaching of their claes;	clothes
Nae herds on *Yarrow's* bonny braes,	shepherds; slopes
Or banks of *Tweed*,	
Delight to chant their hameil lays,	home-bred
Since music's dead.	
At glomin now the bagpipe's dumb,	evening
Whan weary owsen hameward come;	oxen
Sae sweetly as it wont to bum . . .	

Here the nymphs and swains of stanza 3 have become "lasses" and "herds," and the conventional imagery of the first four stanzas has given way to brief glimpses of Scottish life in the old days when folk music was really a part of the daily experience of the common people. The momentary vision of lasses lilting at the bleaching suggests the robust folk quality of the music and the grand out-of-doors atmosphere associated with it; the mention of Yarrow and Tweed, names which are steeped in the traditions of ancient minstrelsy, adds to the suggestive value of the picture. Stanza 6, with its harsh rimes (dumb-come-bum-skreed-hum-dead), completes the descent to reality as Fergusson brings to life the wild martial skirl of the pipes against a background of twilight in the Scottish countryside. The contrast between the style and sound pattern of this stanza and the stiff prettiness of the opening is so startling that we must believe the effect to be intentional.

In the ninth stanza, Fergusson sums up the point of his elegy, attacking the "bastard breed" of "foreign sonnets" which have displaced the "saft-tongu'd melody" of native music (just as the contrasting styles of the "Elegy" itself imply an ironic commentary on the way in which a "bastard breed" of English was taking the place of Scots). Next comes a tribute to the "Birks of Indermay," a beautiful Scots air said to have been the favorite of Fergusson himself, here used as a symbol for all Scottish song:

Cou'd *lav'rocks* at the dawning day,	larks
Cou'd *linties* chirming frae the spray,	linnets warbling
Or todling *burns* that smoothly play	brooks
O'er gowden bed,	golden
Compare wi' *Birks of Indermay?*	
But now they're dead.	

Dr. Wittig, it seems to me, goes too far when he interprets this stanza as a further attack on the Scoto-English style. He does this by printing the stanza with quotation marks not present in Fergusson's text ("Cou'd '*Lav'rocks* at the dawning day,' / Cou'd 'Linties . . .' / Or 'Todling *burns* . . .' ") to suggest that the poet is scornfully mimicking the stereotyped Scoto-English manner in these lines. If such were Fergusson's intention, surely he would have used more obviously hackneyed phrases, such as those in the first part of the "Elegy." As it stands, the stanza has the same kind of delicate charm as stanza 5 and should, I think, be taken at face value. The final stanza, with its urgent patriotic appeal ("Winna your sons"), is stirring and effective as an ending to the poem.

Viewed in this way, the "Elegy on the Death of Scots Music" is a stylistic *tour de force* of great promise. Though the poem has little of the fine spontaneity and swift, natural flow of "The Daft-Days," the "Elegy" shows more imaginative boldness. Fergusson here dares to experiment with two drastically different styles, deftly juxtaposing them to achieve a special satiric point. In so doing, he looks forward to some of the effects in his own later poems (the ending of "The King's Birth-Day," for example) and ultimately to Burn's similar use of shifting styles in "Tam O'Shanter" and other pieces (see note 3). At the same time, apart from its stylistic sophistication, the "Elegy" is a self-conscious expression of the eighteenth-century Scots revivalist spirit, of a culture in danger of being overwhelmed from outside—a culture fighting for its life, so to speak, wishing to preserve intact its ancient heritage and identity.

III "The King's Birth-Day in Edinburgh"

Fergusson's next Scots poem, "The King's Birth-Day in Edinburgh," appeared in *The Weekly Magazine* on the very day that it celebrates, the Fourth of June. The poem must have been written expressly for the occasion, one of the great civic holidays in Edinburgh; and it must have been based on Fergusson's recollections of birthday festivities of the previous year, 1771. This fine poem, in sixteen strikingly original "Habbie" stanzas, represents Fergusson's most ambitious attempt in the vernacular to date as it describes the varied activities of the day: the military and civic ceremonies, the conduct of the City Guard, and the practical joking which went on in the streets on this gay occasion. The theme and structural method are here very like those of "The Daft-Days." As the poet moves rapidly from scene to scene, he observes briefly but vividly many different kinds of activity one after another in order to create a total impression of the crowded and colorful life of the city in holiday mood. This poem, even more than "The Daft-Days," depends upon the cumulative effect achieved through the piling up of individual impressions.

"The King's Birth-Day" opens with one of the most daring, richly humorous passages in Fergusson—if not in all Scottish poetry. He begins by remarking how many poems the Muse has inspired to glorify the birthday celebrations in Edinburgh, but adds, "the limmer's fairly flung" (the hussy is deceived); for the festivities in London are probably just as strenuous and just as glorious "as here at hame," or so Fergusson is "fain to think." On this day, in London as well as in Edinburgh,

. . . fock of ilka age and name,	every
Baith blind and cripple,	both
Forgather aft, O fy for shame!	often
To drink and tipple.	

The comic irony of the exclamation, "O fy for shame!" is brought home in the very next stanza, where the invocation proper begins, and where we find Fergusson himself calling on the Muse for hard liquor:

O *Muse,* be kind, and dinna fash us	do not trouble
To flee awa' beyont Parnassus,	
Nor seek for *Helicon* to wash us,	
That heath'nish spring;	
Wi' Highland whisky scour our hawses,	throats
And gar us sing.	make

These lines probably provided Burns with the suggestion for the bard's song in "The Jolly Beggars": "I never drank the Muse's stank," as well as for passages in "Scotch Drink" (stanzas 1-2) and "Third Epistle to J. Lapraik" (stanza 5).

At any rate, Fergusson's lines are magnificent fun in their own right, and lead directly into the next, even more boldly imaginative, stanza:

Begin then, dame, ye've drunk your fill,	
You woudna hae the tither gill?	other glass
You'll trust me, mair wou'd do you ill,	more
And ding you doitet;	make; stupid
Troth 'twou'd be sair agains my will	sorely
To hae the wyte o't.	blame

The picture of Fergusson buying drinks for the Muse and anxiously warning her against accepting the last glass for fear it will make her tipsy is irresistibly funny. In this brilliant stanza, the humor comes from three sources. In the first place, there is the audacity and ingenuity of the whole concept, the idea of a poet priming the Muse with liquor so as to warm her up for the job at hand, while taking care, at the same time, that she does not get too drunk to function properly. Second, the humor arises out of the incongruity of Fergusson's familiar, not to say cavalier, treatment of a usually dignified and remote abstraction, the poetic muse. He treats this august figure like a barmaid, calling her a "limmer" in stanza 1, which is roughly equivalent to "wench" or "hussy," and buying her drinks in stanza 4. His method here is strikingly akin to that which Burns was to use a few years later in "Address to the Deil" and in "Death and Doctor Hornbook," for Burns adopts the same familiar attitude toward those terrible personages, the devil and death, and achieves precisely the same sort of comic effect. Finally, the stanza, and Fergusson's introduction as a whole, takes on added satiric point when viewed in the light of the artificial English tradition in general. His lines are a droll mockery of the type of poem which begins with a mechanical "invocation" of the muse; they imply a critical repudiation of such wooden devices and a conscious attempt on Fergusson's part to bring poetry back into life.

After this superb introduction, the poem moves briskly forward and, at stanza 5, plunges us immediately into the gay and noisy celebrations of "the Fourth." All the church bells are set ringing; the great castle on the hill overlooking the city is decorated with flags; and at noon the castle guns fire a salute in honor of the royal anniversary. The firing reminds Fergusson of Mons Meg, Scotland's historic piece of ordnance, which, before its removal to London in 1734, had long stood sadly silent on the "King's Bastion" of Edinburgh Castle, for its enormous barrel had been accidentally split generations earlier.[4] In stanza 6, the poet expresses whimsical regret over Meg's impotence:

Oh willawins! MONS MEG, for you,	well-a-day
'Twas firing crack'd thy muckle mou;	big mouth
What black mishanter gart ye spew	mishap made
Baith gut and ga'?	gall
I fear they bang'd thy belly fu'	crammed; full
Against the law.	

The extraordinary vigor and archness of this stanza are self-evident. The last two lines, with their strongly colloquial flavor and sexually ribald overtones, carry the comic personification of the cannon as a woman to its logical conclusion.

In the following passage, Fergusson delivers a stirring tribute to Mons Meg, recalling her ancient and fabulous prowess. Stanza 7 is inimitable and shows Fergusson in his finest vein:

Right seldom am I gi'en to bannin,	swearing
But, by my saul, ye was a cannon,	
Cou'd hit a man, had he been stannin	standing
In shire o' Fife,	
Sax long Scots miles ayont *Clackmannan,*	beyond
And tak his life.	

Here is Fergusson handling the "Habbie" stanza with the most accomplished ease and absolute technical mastery. His lines have the authentic sound of the proud citizen of Edinburgh, spontaneously voicing a somewhat exaggerated tribute to the old cannon. Nothing seems forced or distorted to fit the meter or rime scheme in this passage; it reproduces the natural rhythms of living speech, yet is dramatic in impact and Classic in its perfect regularity of form. This is rare artistry, of a kind that Ramsay at his best could never approach. In re-creating the actual language of the people wedded harmoniously to the exacting discipline of poetic art, Fergusson comes closest to the linguistic magic of Burns.

In stanza 9 we are presented with another vivid little scene, commemorating the ancient custom of pensioning certain privileged beggars called "The King's Bedesmen" (because they were supposed to pray for their royal patron), or, more colloquially, "blue-gown bodies," or "gaberlunzies." Their name and character have been immortalized in the excellent old song, "The Gaberlunzie-man." Every year on the King's Birthday these beggars gathered in Edinburgh from all over Scotland to receive their pay and new suits of clothing.[5] Fergusson characteristically chooses to portray the most amusing part of the whole ceremony, the moment when the beggars change their clothes. They arrive in the most ragged and bedraggled condition imaginable, looking "Like scar-craws new ta'en down frae woodies." But then they quickly "cast their clouted duddies," slip into their fresh new gowns, and get their pay; and the ludicrous transformation is complete, after which—"Than them, what magistrate mair proud is / On king's birth-day?"

After this brief but lively sketch of the "blue-gown bodies," Fergusson goes on to describe in two neatly turned stanzas how the City Guard "gang thro' their functions." On this day the guardsmen are particularly well groomed and powdered in honor of the king, and on that account the more obstreperous folk of Edinburgh take a special delight in pelting them with "clarty unctions" of stones and refuse. Fergusson is always effective when satirizing the Guard; one feels that his heart was in his work. In stanza 11, his mockery of the soldiers is particularly subtle and irresistible when he addresses them with a pathetic plea for mercy and begs them, for Scotland's sake—

Gie not her *bairns* sic deadly pakes, sons; pokes, blows
Nor be sae rude . . .

The next three stanzas on practical joking are fairly well executed and are ingeniously linked. Stanza 12 describes the firework frolics on the streets, and how sometimes a fiery "*serpent*" ignited the "*gizz*" or wig of an elegant passer-by. In the following stanza, Fergusson pictures the owner of the singed wig turning patiently around only to be bowled over by a heavy blow from a dead cat swung, presumably, by some rascally urchin. The mention of dead cats leads directly into stanza 14, where Fergusson warns the "auld wives" of Edinburgh to keep their pets indoors, for the King's Birthday is open season on cats:

If *baudrins* slip but to the door, the cat
I fear, I fear,
She'll no lang shank upon all-four not long walk
This time o' year.

These stanzas, with their impish humor and their attitude of good-natured tolerance, give us vivid glimpses of actual street scenes and characterize in a very short space the variety and abandon of such birthday frolics in Auld Reekie.

In his final two stanzas, Fergusson's "Muse" re-enters the poem; but the reader is startled to discover that it is not the same muse. The alcoholic, sociable goddess of Fergusson's introduction is here abruptly transformed into the dignified conventional muse of English and Scoto-English pastoralism. The violent and bustling scenes of city life are no fit subject for *this* muse, who much prefers the clean countryside where "doggies play, and lambies sport," and where "peerless Fancy hads her court, / And tunes her lays." The metamorphosed muse and insipid neo-Classical diction of this conclusion are, as David Daiches suggests,[6] deliberately ironical. Fergusson brings the freshness and vitality of his poem into sharp focus by ending it on an absurdly conventional note, thus mocking the whole genteel pastoral tradition in poetry (as in the "Elegy on Scots Music") and leaving his reader wishing for more of the hard-drinking muse of the opening stanzas.

"The King's Birth-Day in Edinburgh" shows improvement over "The Daft-Days" in several important respects. Though less firm structurally than "The Daft-Days," the later poem reveals a greater ease, fluency, and technical mastery in handling of the "Habbie" stanza. This improvement, though it is apparent only in certain portions of the poem—notably in the stanzas on Mons Meg—shows that Fergusson was, through the first half of 1772, rapidly gaining control of his medium and was moving toward deeper insight into the subtleties of language and rhythm. In the introductory section, with its richly humorous treatment of the muse, and in the splendid passage on Mons Meg, Fergusson also displays a degree of imaginative power which he had not hitherto achieved.

"The King's Birth-Day" is, moreover, refreshingly original in its treatment of a conventional theme. "Birthday odes," produced by the score throughout the eighteenth century, were usually ceremonial poems, full of dignified and trite compliments to the king and of stereotyped declarations of loyalty. Fergusson's poem is startlingly unlike what we might expect in a "Birthday ode" written to order for the occasion. His treatment is thoroughly undignified; there are no conventional tributes to His Majesty King George III; indeed, the king is not even mentioned. Fergusson is more interested in the lively social aspects of the day—in the barbarous cat-slinging episode, for example—than he is in official compliments. His poem is a comic extravaganza, partly satiric in intention, opening with a magnificent parody of the grandiose invocations which were almost invariably prefixed to "Birthday odes." In short, Fergusson's creative imagination remains entirely unfettered by the dignity of the occasion. The high spirits, the audacity, and the freshness of his treatment are strongly characteristic of Fergusson's usual method and personality.

IV "Caller Oysters"

Fergusson's next Scottish poem, "Caller Oysters" (fresh oysters), is scarcely less original in its conception. It appeared in *The Weekly Magazine* on August 27, twelve weeks after "The King's Birth-Day"; and it describes with humorous abandon the joys of the approaching oyster season.

"Caller Oysters" is written in the six-line stanza, but in theme and treatment it seems to be unrelated to earlier Scottish poetry. Its immediate inspiration appears to have been an English poem,

John Philips' clever parody "The Splendid Shilling," the first four lines of which Fergusson prefixed as the motto of his poem.[7] But, although the germinal idea came from Philips, "Caller Oysters" is, in other respects, an entirely independent poem, and one which was to exert a very specific influence over Burns. For instance, Fergusson's tenth stanza (with its scorn of "glakit fools" who "pamper their weyms wi' fousom trash") undoubtedly suggested Burns's expression of the same sentiment in "To a Haggis," while the "hobble-coble-noble" rimes in Fergusson's first stanza are clearly echoed in Burns's "Auld Farmer's Salutation" (stanza 7).

"Caller Oysters" opens with three impressive stanzas praising the Firth of Forth as a bountiful source of fish and various sea foods, but especially of new oysters in September. Fergusson's first stanza, with its consciously formal note, makes an effective beginning:

Of a' the waters that can hobble — toss, move
A fishin yole or salmon coble, — flat-bottomed boat
And can reward the fishers trouble,
Or south or north,
There's nane sae spacious and sae noble
As Firth o' *Forth.*

Here the slightly artificial tone of line 3 seems appropriate, though one feels that this tone is pushed too far in the "Or . . . or" construction of the next line, which smacks of neo-Classical jargon and is a shade too formal to be assimilated in this context. On the whole, however, Fergusson succeeds admirably in achieving the combination of dignity and gentle humor that he is aiming at in this ceremonial tribute to the Forth. In the next stanza, such lines as "The eil fou souple wags her tail," and "Their spindle-shanks the labsters trail," with their curious fullness of detail, reinforce the mood of quiet humor, while the reference in stanza 3 to the time of year is skillfully brought in to effect the transition from fish in general to oysters in particular. The poem was written late in August, just before the beginning of the oyster season in September, when "Auld Reikie's sons" will enjoy

New oysters fresh;
The halesomest and nicest gear — wholesomest; fare
Of fish or flesh.

In these vigorous lines Fergusson introduces his theme and brings the opening section of his poem to an effective close.

The next three stanzas deal with the medicinal qualities of oysters. The opening words of stanza 4, "O! then," refer back to "September's merry month" in stanza 3, and they make an extremely natural transition. At stanza 4, there is a marked increase in the tempo of the verse and in the intensity of feeling, as Fergusson begins to warm up to his subject:

O! then we needna gie a plack	small coin
For dand'ring mountebank or quack,	wandering
Wha o' their drogs sae bauldly crack,	boldly talk
And spred sic notions,	such
As gar their feckless patients tak	feeble
Their stinkin potions.	

These lines, with their incisive expression of scorn and indignation, are brilliantly executed. They have a strong colloquial expressivess, the naturalness of living speech. The harsh rimes, "plack," "quack," "crack," and "tak," snap like whips at the end of each line, giving the stanza tightness of structure without impairing the smooth development of thought. The very sound of these words reinforces the feeling of scorn and disgust, a feeling further intensified in the last line by the ugly word "stinkin," which should be given great emphasis in reading.

The stanza which follows these excellent lines is, to me, the weakest in the poem. Its excessively tricky rimes and tortured grammar give an impression of laboriousness and of overstrained effects which clashes jarringly with the simple, direct, and powerful expression of the preceding passage. In stanza 6, however, there is an immediate recovery of power, where Fergusson whimsically recommends oysters as a sovereign cure for "plouky [pimply] noses" in drunkards. Such lines as the third, in which the poet urges tipplers to "Fling owr your craig [throat] sufficient doses," typify the vigorous comic flow of this stanza.

In the next group of three stanzas, Fergusson is equally effective. His consideration of the curative value of oysters leads him naturally to reflect affectionately upon the coziness and friendliness of his favorite Edinburgh oyster cellar, Luckie Middlemist's in the Cowgate, and upon the physical and spiritual refreshment he has found there. On rainy days he finds this haunt particularly attractive:

Whan big as burns the gutters rin,	brooks; run
Gin ye hae catcht a droukit skin,	if; drenched
To *Luckie Middlemist's* loup in,	leap
And sit fu snug	
O'er oysters and a dram o' gin,	
Or haddock lug.	ear

In this and the next two stanzas, Fergusson is obviously describing his own pleasant experiences at Luckie Middlemist's. The passage is interesting for the light it throws both on the poet's social habits in particular and on Edinburgh tavern life in general. We learn that Fergusson often "louped in" to Luckie's during the wet and chilly September weather for a snack of oysters or fish and for a warming glass of gin. The stanzas are aglow with a sense of Fergusson's huge and hearty enjoyment of the snug, sociable atmosphere of the place, with its comfortable "*ingle* cheek," its rousing good fellowship, and "gude fare." The stark contrast between Luckie Middlemist's and his own comfortless lodgings is suggested rather wistfully in the last lines of this section:

I trow there was nae hame to seek	
Whan steghin there.	gorging

It is in such vivid little sketches of Edinburgh life that Fergusson's style shows to best advantage. With his keen eye for concrete detail and with his wonderfully expressive command of the vernacular, he is able to reveal in a few brief lines the whole reality of the scene and to suggest with striking clarity and precision its characteristic atmosphere and feeling. This ability is Fergusson's greatest gift as a poet.

Stanza 10, deriding the "glakit fools, o'er rife o' cash," who pamper themselves with elaborate meals of "fousom trash," has already been noted in connection with Burns's "To a Haggis." The stanza is written with great force and zest. The dramatic contrast between the finicky aristocrat and the sturdy "chiel" (fellow) who "gusts his gabb [flavors his mouth] wi' oyster sauce" is very effective. The latter alliterative phrase, with its strong, earthy quality suggestive of healthy and uninhibited appetite, helps to drive home the humorous point of the contrast.

The next two stanzas together present another pleasant glimpse of Edinburgh social life. They are, however, less detailed and less intimate than the stanzas on Luckie Middlemist's and, therefore, less vivid. They describe a custom, popular among the young lads of Fergusson's time, of taking Sunday evening excursions with their "*joes*" to the neighboring fishing towns of Musselbrough and Newhaven. Here the lads would treat their sweethearts to fresh oysters or "*mussel brose,*" sometimes followed by hard liquor just to "weet their wizen" (throat). Fergusson comments archly that the lads usually felt compelled to "swallow o'er a dainty soup, / For fear they gizzen" (swallow a small mouthful, for fear they parch with dryness). The mention of liquor in combination with oysters leads directly into the final brilliant stanza:

A' ye wha canna stand sae sicker,	steadily
Whan twice you've toom'd the big ars'd bicker,	emptied; drinking bowl
Mix *caller oysters* wi' your liquor,	
And I'm your debtor,	
If greedy *priest* or drouthy *vicar*	thirsty
Will thole it better.	endure

With this bit of humorous advice, and with a playful thrust at the hard-drinking Scottish clergy, Fergusson most fittingly ends his poem. Many of the Scottish churchmen, such as the notorious Dr. Alexander Webster, were noted for their drinking capacity; and here Fergusson slyly sets them up as a criterion against which any man's alcoholic prowess may fairly be judged.

"Caller Oysters" is, on the whole, a creditable performance. The subject itself is daringly original; few poets of Fergusson's time would have dared to break so boldly with tradition in writing a poem about so lowly a subject as oysters. In his choice of such a subject from common everyday life, Fergusson anticipates Burns and, ultimately, Wordsworth. Though the poem never rises to the heights of brilliance that Fergusson achieved in parts of "The King's Birth-day," it is consistently good. In this poem, Fergusson's blunders are fewer, his hand is steadier. "Caller Oysters" marks a further step in his swift development as a creative artist, this time in the direction of firmness and maturity of technique.

V *Two Epistles*

In *The Weekly Magazine* on September 3, just one week after the publication of "Caller Oysters," there appeared a poetic epistle "To Mr. Robert Fergusson," signed "J. S., *Berwick, Aug. 31.*" And in the very next issue of the magazine, on Thursday, September 10, appeared Fergusson's "Answer to Mr. J. S.'s Epistle," his fifth Scots poem of 1772, and his first attempt at the poetic epistle.

Both J. S.'s epistle and Fergusson's answer are modeled on the famous poetical correspondence of 1719 in the "Habbie" stanza between William Hamilton of Gilbertfield and Allan Ramsay.[8] J. S. follows the line of Hamilton's first letter to Ramsay in particular, where Hamilton is writing to a poet whom he admires, whom he has never met, but whose acquaintance he wishes to cultivate. In both cases, the circumstances and the purpose in writing are identical.[9] J. S., like Hamilton, expresses the desire to meet and drink with the poet he admires. Both poems open with a eulogy and end with a trick subscription in the last stanza. The answers of Ramsay and of Fergusson to these epistles present interesting points of comparison and contrast. Fergusson's reply, like Ramsay's, is cordial in tone, returns the invitation to "foregather," and ends by wishing his correspondent health, happiness, and long life. On the other hand, Fergusson's reaction to praise is strikingly different from Ramsay's. Ramsay egotistically accepts Hamilton's extravagant eulogy with good grace, as though he felt it his due; Fergusson, however, rejects J. S.'s more moderate praise as the rankest flattery.

Fergusson's answer begins with a very spirited passage, humorously berating J. S. as a flatterer:

I trou, my mettl'd Louden lathie,	Lothian lad
Auld farran birky I maun ca' thee,	old-fashioned clever fellow; must
For whan in gude black print I saw thee	
Wi' souple gab,	mouth
I skirl'd fou loud, "Oh wae befa' thee!	cried; woe
But thou'rt a daub."	expert ("dab")
Awa', ye wylie fleetchin *fallow* . . .	wily; flattering

This grand opening, with its sprightliness, its mock indignation, and its richly humorous conversational tone, is easily the best part of the epistle. Fergusson here strikes a perfect balance: he firmly rejects J. S.'s "butter'd words," but does so in such a friendly and good-natured way that J. S. could not possibly be offended. He manages to give the impression that, although he does not believe what J. S. has said, he is, nevertheless, pleased with the letter. J. S. could not have been anything but delighted with the verve and sparkle of these opening stanzas of Fergusson's reply. The phrase "auld farran birky" (old-fashioned clever fellow) strikes the keynote of familiar witticism, while the last line, "But thou'rt a daub," beautifully clinches the meaning of the stanza, and brings it to a strong natural climax.

The rest of Fergusson's epistle is competently and smoothly written, with only occasional brilliant touches. Stanza 7, for example, is finely conceived and executed. The opening exclamation, "Hch lad!" helps to build up the familiar and cordial atmosphere of the letter as a whole, while it serves as a natural prelude to the rather wistful expression of regret which follows. Stanza 13 is equally attractive:

Tho' jillet Fortune scoul and quarrel,	fickle girl
And keep me frae a bien beef barrel,	prosperous
As lang's I've twopence i' the warl',	
I'll ay be vockie	glad
To part a *fadge* or *girdle farl*	flat wheaten loaf;
Wi' Louden Jockie.	griddled oatcake

This stanza, with its warm-hearted sentiment and easy, fluent style, is at least equal to anything in the Hamilton-Ramsay letters.

The "Answer to Mr. J. S.'s Epistle" taken as a whole, though not one of Fergusson's better poems artistically, is yet a significant milestone in his development. It is his first attempt at the rimed epistle and, judged as such, is a very promising performance. The poem shows that Fergusson was certainly familiar with the traditional models for this genre. He had probably studied the Hamilton-Ramsay correspondence with some care; and this first attempt of Fergusson's compares favorably with theirs. Although it would be easy to pick out many individual stanzas in the letters of Hamilton and Ramsay which are as effective as anything in Fergusson's poem, it would be hard to find a single epistle which is as consistently good throughout as this one of Fergusson. His "Answer," then, may be evaluated as superior on the whole to its models, though perhaps only slightly so. Fergusson's contribution to the rimed epistle tradidition is chiefly in the direction of smoother technique: he uses fewer strained rimes and distorted constructions than Hamilton or Ramsay, and his stanzas give an impression of greater spontaneity and naturalness of expression. In this respect, he paved the way for the excellent epistles of Burns, many of which are strikingly reminiscent of Fergusson's style. Finally, the epistle is noticeably free from the typical weaknesses of which we have remarked in his earlier Scottish poems: looseness in structure and the introduction of jarring neo-Classicisms and feeble generalities.

The "Answer to J. S." is of further interest for the light it throws on Fergusson's attitude toward himself as a poet at this stage in his career. Whereas the glowing letter of J. S. is positive proof that popular recognition of Fergusson as a new national poet was enthusiastic and almost instantaneous, Fergusson's reaction, as we have seen, was excessively modest. He scoffs (stanzas 3-5) at the notion that his poor verses should be ranked with those of Ramsay, or even those of the feeble Pennecuik. He looks up to Ramsay as possessing genius of the first order, but he himself has only "a knack, / To gar auld-warld wordies clack / In hamespun rhime." Fergusson's attitude is here, no doubt, absolutely sincere, and understandable enough in a young poet of twenty-two. After all, Fergusson had published only four Scots pieces thus far; he was, according to all the early biographers, modest by nature; and he did not yet feel at all sure of himself despite his initial success with these poems. But, as time went on, he was to grow rapidly in self-confidence and in the realization of his own extraordinary powers. It is instructive at this point to look ahead some nine months to his second and last verse-letter which reveals a marked change in attitude.

Fergusson's second epistle appeared, not in *The Weekly Magazine,* but in a provincial paper, *The Perth Magazine of Knowledge and Pleasure,* on July 2, 1773. It was addressed to one "Andrew Gray" who, in a previous issue of *The Perth Magazine* (June 11), had published a laudatory verse-letter to Fergusson.[10] These epistles between Andrew Gray and Fergusson are, of course, slight occasional pieces, very similar in content, tone, and level of performance to the "J. S." letters and, like them, fall squarely within the Hamilton-Ramsay tradition. But there are points of special interest in them. Andrew Gray in his original epistle (a second appeared on September 17, 1773, after Fergusson's reply) voices enthusiastic praise of Fergusson's choice of Scots as a poetic medium—praise which is indicative of a widespread sentimental attachment to the vernacular among Scotsmen who were eager for new poetry in the old, expressive mother tongue, and who were, therefore, delighted with Fergusson's brilliant work. In his reply, Fergusson characterizes Andrew as a smooth flatterer ("A soupler or mair fletching loun,/ Ne'er hap'd on hurdies") just as he had done before in his "Answer to J. S.," but here his rejection of praise is noticeably more moderate than in the earlier epistle:

Can ye nae ither theme divine	
To blaw upon, but *my* engyne?	genius
At *nature* keek, she's unco fine	look; very
Redd up, and braw;	neat, smart
And can gie scouth to *muses nine*	scope
At *Whistle-ha*.	
Her road awhile is rough an' round,	
An' few poetic gowans found;	daisies
The stey braes o' the muses ground	steep slopes
We scarce can crawl up;	
But on the tap we're light as wind	top
To scour an' gallop.	run

In this passage, Fergusson places significant emphasis on the hard work and long apprenticeship necessary in the making of a good poet. This comment on hard work and "weary practice" (stanza 8) serves to refute those critics who, misled by the carefree atmosphere of many of Fergusson's poems, represent him as a careless and hasty poet with a lucky sort of knack for hitting on the right word, the precise idiom. These lines, no doubt, reflect Fergusson's own experience, and suggest that he worked hard on his poetry, took it seriously, and was very much concerned with finished craftsmanship. Indeed, a large majority of his Scots poems show the result of this "weary practice" in their careful and conscious artistry. By this time Fergusson had some fifteen or sixteen successful Scots poems behind him, and in this epistle his increasing sureness and confidence in his own strength are clearly apparent. He had made the long hard climb to poetic mastery, and was ready to "scour an' gallop."

VI "Braid Claith"

But, at the time of his reply to J. S. in September of 1772, Fergusson had not as yet achieved this kind of assurance. In the two months which followed, however, he was to make tremendous strides forward. Whatever the "Answer to J. S." may have lacked in brilliancy and originality was immediately made up for in Fergusson's next Scots poem, "Braid Claith" (broad cloth). This poem, Fergusson's first pure satire in the vernacular and his most perfect single piece to date, appeared on October 15 in *The Weekly Magazine*, just five weeks after the epistle. "Braid Claith," a comparatively short poem, consists of nine "Habbie" stanzas and deals with the common human tendency to judge a man not according to his real merit, but by the shabbiness or elegance of his clothing. Fergusson uses the phrase "braid claith" as a symbol for expensive, fashionable garments of any kind.

Fergusson's theme is, of course, a universal one; but in the details of expression and presentation he owes nothing, so far as I can discover, to earlier poetry.[11] The theme was a congenial one to Burns, too, as might be expected; his "To a Louse," for example, has a similar moral, and he may very well have had "Braid Claith" in mind when he wrote the fourth stanza of his "Epistle to Kennedy," though his point of view is somewhat different from Fergusson's and his attitude more belligerent.

Of all Fergusson's works, "Braid Claith" is the most tightly and carefully organized. The poem is extremely simple and clear-cut in design and relentlessly logical in its swift development. The very simplicity of its structure and the directness of its method have much to do with the extraordinary power of this little poem. There are no digressions, no side-glances in "Braid Claith"; Fergusson goes straight to the point, and sticks to it with a tenacity which, for him, is unusual. The poem falls into three main divisions: in his first three stanzas, Fergusson presents a masterly exposition of his theme; in stanzas 4 to 7, he develops it with two graphic illustrations; and, in the last two stanzas, he sums up his philosophy of clothes in a way which, as William Roughead remarks,[12] must have delighted the soul of Thomas Carlyle.

Too much has been made of the biographical significance of "Braid Claith," especially by Frederick C. Green.[13] When he speaks of the "unusual bitterness" and "cynicism" of the poem, Green is surely misinterpreting the spirit of this piece. "Braid Claith" is a realistic poem, surprisingly mature in outlook, and restrained in expression. It implies a harsher indictment of society than is usual in Fergusson. In it we miss the sunny atmosphere, the carefree gaiety of "The Daft-Days," "The King's Birth-Day," or "Caller Oysters." The poem reflects Fergusson's more serious observations of men and manners; and, no doubt, it also reflects in a general way his own hard experience. "Braid Claith" is the expression of a man who has no illusions about life. But there is no bitterness, no cynicism; rather, the poem reveals an attitude of realistic acceptance of human frailty. As Hugh Walker says, Fergusson "states facts without rating the world for being what it is." [14]

In his opening stanza Fergusson goes straight to the heart of his theme:

Ye wha are fain to hae your name
Wrote in the bonny book of fame,
Let merit nae pretension claim
　　To laurel'd wreath,
But hap ye weel, baith back and wame, 　　　cover; belly
　　In gude Braid Claith.

These lines are beautifully executed. There is a constant repetition of the open "a" sound in the words "fain," "name," "hae," "fame," "nae," "claim," "wreath" (pronounced "wraith"), "baith," "wame," "Braid," and "Claith." And this assonance not only gives the stanza tightness, neatness, and unity of tone, but adds to its tricksy satiric quality. The internal rime in the first line, combined with the alliteration in "fain . . . fame" and "bonny book," creates a clever, comic effect which is maintained throughout the poem. Fergusson's last line, "In gude Braid Claith," is a refrain which is repeated at the end of each stanza, with variations only in the preposition. The refrain is very effective, since it not only serves as a firm structural bond, but also acts, with its heavy spondaic movement, as a sort of "punch line," driving home the satiric point of each stanza. This refrain idea was probably suggested to Fergusson by the "But now he's dead" formula of the comic-elegy tradition.

In his next two contrasting stanzas Fergusson develops his theme. He comments first on the social success of the man who is dapperly dressed in "gude Braid Claith"; and then, in stanza 3, he pities the plight of the poor man who cannot afford such finery, for he is "A chiel that ne'er will be respekit." Fergusson is here using a method of dramatic contrast which he continues to employ throughout the poem. In addition, he uses such devices as alliteration, assonance, consonance, and trick rime with unusual frequency. For example, in stanza 2 the line, "Bids bauld to bear the gree awa'," is notable both for its alliteration and for its strongly idiomatic quality. These devices tend to give a witty tone to his style and to counteract any suggestion of bitterness in the satire. The quaintly colloquial phrasing, with quietly humorous overtones, which is typical of all Fergusson's Scots poems, helps further to create this distinctive and witty effect in "Braid Claith."

Having completed the exposition of his theme in general terms, Fergusson illustrates it in stanzas 4 and 5 with a brilliant sketch of the "barber spark." Here his rich comic observation comes into play once more:

On Sabbath-days the barber spark,	
Whan he has done wi' scrapin wark,	
Wi' siller broachie in his sark,	silver; shirt
Gangs trigly, faith!	sprucely
. . . .	
Weel might ye trow, to see them there,	
That they to shave your haffits bare,	cheeks
Or curl an' sleek a pickle hair,	little
Wou'd be right laith,	loath
Whan pacing wi' a gawsy air	stately, portly
In gude Braid Claith.	

Fergusson pokes satiric fun at the ludicrous vanity of the barber as a type by emphasizing the contrast between his everyday work and his pretentious Sunday afternoon promenading. He reveals the shallowness of the man's character through the suggestion that on such occasions the barber would be ashamed of his occupation. His fine clothes enable him to pretend he is something which he is not. Fergusson makes the constrast between the pretense and the reality vivid and memorable by his skillful choice of details: on the one side, he has the "siller broachie" and the "gawsy air"; on the other, the shaving, curling, sleeking, and "scrapin wark."

In stanzas 6 and 7, Fergusson presents another concrete illustration of his central theme. Here again he employs the method of dramatic contrast, showing how largely success or failure in love-making depends upon the stylishness or shabbiness of the lover's dress. The phrase, "crook her bonny mou' fu' sair," it should be noted, was a traditional expression signifying a lady's disdain. It occurs often in the popular ballads and is another example of Fergusson's effective use of semi-proverbial phrases. On the whole, however, the two stanzas on the lover are less vivid than the passage on the barber simply because they are not so rich in power of suggestion through specific detail.

The two concluding stanzas of "Braid Claith" bring the poem to a fitting, powerful culmination. Having illustrated how people attach a false importance to the quality of one's clothing, Fergusson summarizes brilliantly in his eighth stanza:

Braid Claith lends fock an unco heese, — wonderful lift
Makes mony kail-worms butter-flies,
Gies mony a doctor his degrees
    For little skaith: — expense
In short, you may be what you please
    Wi' gude Braid Claith.

The pleasing cumulative force of these parallel constructions and the comic reference to human "kail-worms" and "butter-flies" (a thought, by the way, which Fergusson was to pick up and develop later in his "On Seeing a Butterfly in the Street") give the stanza lightness and imaginative spark without detracting from its strong, satiric point. In his final stanza, Fergusson maintains this mode of expression, but he sharpens the cutting edge of his satire for a last incisive thrust. His transition from stanza 8 is smooth and natural:

For thof ye had as wise a snout on — although

As *Shakespeare* or Sir *Isaac Newton,*
Your judgment fouk wou'd hae a doubt on,
I'll tak my aith, oath
Till they cou'd see ye wi' a suit on
O' gude Braid Claith.

Fergusson's trick rimes are here, as in stanza 3, extremely effective in striking a perfect balance between humorous expression and pointed, satiric meaning.

Viewed as a whole and in relation to Fergusson's development, "Braid Claith" is a memorable poem. Here again, as in "Caller Oysters," his choice of subject from the life around him is unusual for the time in which he was writing. In this poem, "braid claith" becomes a symbol not merely for fine clothes but for a whole social attitude. In attacking the attitude itself, Fergusson, with a fine artistic sense, focusses attention on fashionable "braid claith" as a tangible, outward manifestation of the attitude. This method of concretizing his theme is, in itself, evidence of Fergusson's sensitive poetic imagination and is proof that Fergusson, consciously or not, knew how to control his readers' response, "braid claith" being a prime example of T. S. Eliot's "objective correlative" at work. The poem shows a maturity of mind, a depth of insight into characters and manners which Fergusson's pen had not hitherto revealed; and, at the same time, it is executed with admirable skill and artistry.

"Braid Claith" shows Fergusson in a new light: it proves that he was something more than a clever versifier, than a lighthearted boy with a lucky gift for rendering vivid sketches of Edinburgh life. It shows him rather as a thoughtful and consciously creative artist, not merely portraying scenes in the life around him for their own sakes, but carefully selecting and moulding his materials and arranging them according to a unified, logical pattern to create a single and powerful impact upon the mind of his reader. "Braid Claith" is different from any of Fergusson's earlier poems in the firmness and simplicity of its organization. Although it has nothing of the lighthearted abandon or sweeping descriptive method of such poems as "The Daft-Days" and "The King's Birth-Day," nevertheless, with its Classic perfection of form, and its single-minded serious purpose, "Braid Claith" shows Fergusson as a more mature and thoughtful artist than he had been in any of his earlier works.

VII *Two Scots Pastorals*

Just two weeks after the appearance of "Braid Claith" Fergusson's first Scottish pastoral, "An Eclogue to the Memory of Dr. William Wilkie, late Professor of Natural Philosophy in the University of St Andrews," was published in *The Weekly Magazine* of October 29. This poem is written in competent heroic couplets; and, with the possible exception of "An Eclogue," which cannot be precisely dated, it represents Fergusson's first use of this form for a Scottish poem and (not counting the paraphrase of Horace) his first departure from the "Habbie" stanza. Fergusson's eclogue is very closely related to the tradition of modern Scottish pastoralism originated by Allan Ramsay; indeed, it is directly modeled on two of Ramsay's pastorals. For the structure and thematic development of his poem, Fergusson is heavily indebted to Ramsay's eclogue, "Richy and Sandy: On the Death of Mr. Addison" (1721), and for several of his details to Ramsay's "Robert, Richy, and Sandy: A Pastoral on the Death of Matthew Prior" (1728). The poem consists of a dialogue between two shepherds, Geordie and Davie, who are mourning the loss of their comrade, Fergusson's old teacher and close personal friend, William Wilkie.

The grief which Fergusson is trying to express for his old St. Andrews friend, the eccentric author of *The Epigoniad,* was no doubt perfectly sincere and heartfelt. Unfortunately, however, Fergusson's sincerity, the deep personal sorrow that he must have experienced at Wilkie's death, is only momentarily apparent in his poem; for the most part, his sincerity of feeling is smothered by the artificiality of his medium. He imitates here the traditional style of Ramsay's pastoralism, a style characterized by a judicious blend of the natural and the conventional. Now, Fergusson, it must be admitted, succeeds remarkably well in recreating this Scottish pastoral manner: his performance, especially in his deft handling of the heroic couplet, is certainly superior to Ramsay's. But the pastoral convention is notoriously ill-suited to the expression of real personal grief. Fergusson is forced by the convention to write in terms of "shepherd swains" and "bonny lambies"; and, in following Ramsay too closely, he becomes involved in much of the stereotyped pastoral diction which Ramsay absorbed from English pastoralism; consequently, although the "Eclogue on Wilkie" contains some vigorous Scots phrasing and some fine natural touches, it gives an overall impression of disturbing artificiality. Some passages have a sort of superficial prettiness which is utterly out of keeping with the expression of sincere grief. Fergusson is struggling to break with the conventions of "polite" or genteel literature, to develop his own literary personality, and yet to remain within eighteenth-century poetic tradition in order to be accepted by the public as a serious poet. This struggle can be traced throughout Fergusson's career; as he gains more self-confidence, he moves further and further away from the conventions of each genre he attempts, and he becomes an increasingly mature and original poet. In this first essay at the pastoral elegy, however, he sticks fairly close to the accepted style in such poems, and the personal note is only occasionally sounded.

The way in which this natural-artificial style works at cross-purposes with the personal sentiment of the poem may be illustrated by a few lines chosen almost at random:

To weet wi' hallow'd draps his sacred bier,
Whase sangs will ay in Scotland be rever'd,
While *slow-gawn owsen* turn the flow'ry swaird; slow-going oxen
While bonny *lambies* lick the dews of spring,
While *gaudsmen* whistle, or while birdies sing. plowboys

The introduction here of such hackneyed phrases associated with pastoralism as "sacred bier," "flow'ry swaird," "bonny lambies," "dews of spring," and "birdies sing," strikes a decidedly false note. Fergusson's use of such woodenly pretty phrases gives the whole poem an overly conventional cast. On the other hand, the poem is filled with vivid details of farm life. These homely touches, of course, clash with the neo-Classical elements, as, for example, in the lines quoted above the "slow-gawn owsen" clashes with the "flow'ry swaird." These inappropriate expressions crop up in passages which are otherwise very effective: the word "supplies" in "The ingle-nook supplies the simmer fields" weakens a splendid description of winter on the farm; the phrase "delight the view," mars the fine passage on Wilkie's agricultural improvements.

The most attractive passage in the eclogue comes near the end, in the last speech of Davie, praising Wilkie's astronomical lore:

They tell me, Geordie, he had sic a gift — such
That scarce a starnie blinkit frae the lift, — star; sky
But he wou'd some auld warld name for't find,
As gart him keep it freshly in his mind: — made
For this some ca'd him an uncanny wight; — called
The clash gaed round, "he had the second sight;" — gossip
A tale that never fail'd to be the pride
Of grannies spinnin at the ingle side.

It will be noted that there is absolutely no pastoral jargon in these lines. The passage has a quality of intimacy, a quiet charm which shows what Fergusson might have done had he been able to shake himself free from the Ramsay tradition.

Fergusson did much better, however, with "An Eclogue," the other pastoral which he wrote in 1772, and in which he emancipated himself more or less completely from the influence of Allan Ramsay. This poem cannot be dated accurately since it never appeared in *The Weekly Magazine* and was not published until early in 1773 when it was included among the nine Scottish pieces in Fergusson's volume of *Poems*. Since this volume was prepared by Fergusson during the last month or two of 1772, "An Eclogue" is almost certainly a product of that year— probably of the fall of 1772, judging from its relative maturity. At any rate, it seems best to take it up here, since the poem presents significant points of comparison and contrast with the "Eclogue on Wilkie."

"An Eclogue" is a humorous duologue between two farmers, "Sandie" and "Willie," on the age-old folk theme of the henpecked husband. A fresh and unsophisticated poem, full of realistic detail, it seems to be more akin to the older tradition of Scottish pastoralism than to the eighteenth-century Ramsayesque variety. It is reminiscent, in the robust quality of its humor and in its kind of details, of such masterpieces as Henryson's "Robin and Makyne" and as the anonymous "Wife of Auchtermuchty." Like them, it portrays rural life and character from the point of view of an amused spectator or eavesdropper. At the same time, the poem is strikingly different from the "Eclogue on Wilkie" and from any of Ramsay's pastorals: it is totally free of neo-Classical diction and of the stale conventions which one expects to find in eighteenth-century pastoral poetry. Here Fergusson's peasants are not gentlemen in disguise; they give the impression of being real farmers. The conversation of Sandie and Willie is uaffected and down to earth; it develops with the utmost naturalness; and it ends just as we might expect such a chat to end in real life. Fergusson's complete break with the artificial Ramsay tradition in this fine eclogue undoubtedly helped prepare the way for Burns's realistic use of the eclogue form in such poems as "The Twa Dogs."

Fergusson's execution of this poem is masterly. He writes in the conventional heroic couplet, but does not allow this metrical form to become too obtrusive. Only about half of the couplets are closed, and Fergusson handles them in such a way that they do not interfere with the easy conversational flow of the verse. A few lines from Willie's first speech will illustrate this point:

Our beasties here will take their e'ening pluck,	
An' now sin Jock's gane hame the byres to muck,	cowhouses; clean
Fain wou'd I houp my friend will be inclin'd	hope
To gie me a' the secrets o' his mind:	
Heh! Sandie, lad, what dool's come owr ye now,	sorrow; over
That you to whistle ne'er will crook your mou.	mouth

Fergusson gives his poem a rich, earthy flavor by constant reference to the ordinary objects of farm life expressed in racy vernacular idiom. The eclogue is filled with such homely phrases as: "loos'd their sair toil'd owsen frae the pleugh," "ca'd [drove] their cattle to the town" (farmstead), "Sandie thus began the cracks" (conversation), "tuneless puddocks [frogs] croakin i' the boggs," "byres to muck," "nor faush your thumb," "kirnstaff . . . gizzand" (churnstaff . . . dried out), "cheese-rack toom" (empty), "hair-mould [mouldy] milk," "ferra cow" (cow missing calf), "braw reek rising frae my lum" (chimney), and so forth. This kind of diction is a far cry indeed from the shallow prettiness of eighteenth-century English pastoralism and even from the Scottish pastoral manner of Ramsay. Ramsay had never dared to go so far in the direction of realism; the watered down language of his *Gentle Shepherd,* for example, appears tame in comparison with Fergusson's robust diction in this extraordinary pastoral eclogue.

"An Eclogue" has many delightfully natural touches in it,

such as the passage where Willie gives his opinion on the subject of tea. His naïve suspicion of it as something new, foreign, and expensive is, of course, perfectly typical of his class:

I mind mysell, it's nae sae lang sin syne,	since then
When Auntie Marion did her stamack tyne,	stomach lose
That *Davs* our gardiner came frae *Apple-bogg*,	
An' gae her tea to tak by way o' drog.	drug

It may be noted that this passage also suggests how extremely limited was Willie's experience with tea, the sinister "drog" on which he comments so knowingly. The charm of the eclogue lies largely in such fine human touches and shrewd insight into peasant character. The speech of Sandie, which immediately follows these lines, is irresistibly humorous:

Whan ilka herd for cauld his fingers rubbs,	shepherd
An' cakes o' ice are seen upo' the dubbs;	puddles
At morning, whan frae pleugh or fauld I come,	plow; fold
I'll see a braw reek rising frae my lum,	smoke; chimney
An' ablins think to get a rantin blaze	maybe; roaring
To fley the frost awa' an' toast my taes;	frighten; toes
But whan I shoot my nose in, ten to ane	
If I weelfardly see my ane hearthstane;	with a welcome
She round the ingle with her gimmers sits,	gossips
Crammin their gabbies wi' her nicest bits,	mouths
While the gudeman out-by maun fill his crap	outside must; crop
Frae the milk coggie, or the parritch cap.	dish; porridge bowl

Sandie's indignation and injured feelings at this treatment are skillfully brought out here, especially in the last couplet where he refers to himself as the "gudeman"—as the husband, breadwinner, and master of the house, who cannot even get to sit by his own fireside.

"An Eclogue" shows an easy familiarity with country life, which is surprising when we consider that Fergusson spent most of his life in the city of Edinburgh. He had, of course, seen something of agricultural life around St. Andrews, during afternoon rambles and, more especially, during week-end visits at the nearby farm of William Wilkie. And he had twice visited his uncle John Forbes in Aberdeenshire for extended periods. Finally, there were his frequent week-end excursions into the countryside around his native city. Edinburgh was a fairly small town by modern standards, crowded together within very narrow limits, and open to the country on all sides. A few minutes' walk would have brought Fergusson into the open fields and farmlands, and he seems to have taken full advantage of this fact.

At any rate, his poetry shows that his keenly observant eye made the most of these limited opportunities. He could write about rural life and characters with ease and absolute confidence because he intuitively knew that life, city-bred though he was. He had the kind of imaginative insight which every good poet possesses—the ability to observe details of life and characters, and from them to sense the whole. In "An Eclogue" he created two country types which are thoroughly real and convincing, and he presented them against a background of farm life and problems which is unmistakably authentic. The more one reads the poem, the more he is impressed with the intimacy of mood and the wealth of vivid detail. "An Eclogue" rings true: it portrays the everyday experiences of country folks as they really are, and yet it does this artistically and dramatically. The poem is a little masterpiece of realistic description and shrewd characterization, and these qualities contrast sharply with the usual artificialities of the pastoral tradition.

"An Eclogue" is a far better poem than the "Eclogue on Wilkie." It represents a new and brilliant development in eighteenth-century Scottish poetry, and it leads directly to Burns. "An Eclogue" is, in fact, the first modern Scottish pastoral which, while conforming to tradition in the matter of form and meter, boldly violates all the conventional patterns in its characters, situation, sentiments, and language. In thus daring to swim against the current and to explore new paths, Fergusson showed that in these last months of 1772 he was rapidly attaining artistic maturity and self-confidence.

VIII "Hallow-fair"

This growing confidence and maturity are abundantly evident in Fergusson's next poem, his most ambitious to date, "Hallow-fair," published in Ruddiman's periodical on November 12, just two weeks after the "Eclogue on Wilkie." "Hallow-fair" is written in the "Christis Kirk" stanza—Fergusson's first use of this form—

and is another lively description of social activity, the goings-on at a market which was held annually in November near Edinburgh.

"Hallow-fair" belongs to the pure tradition of "Christis Kirk," and is related in a general way to all of the earlier poems in that special genre: "Christis Kirk on the Green"; "Peblis to the Play"; Alexander Scott's "Justing and Debait"; "The Blythsome Bridal"; Ramsay's sequels to "Christis Kirk"; John Skinner's "Monymusk Christmas Ba'ing"; and so forth.[15] In its subject, however, and in its choice of detail "Hallow-fair" is most nearly akin to "Peblis." The "Christis Kirk" genre was an ideal medium of expression for Fergusson, since it called for the lively, swift-paced method of description at which he was already adept. The experience he had gained in "The Daft-Days" and in "The King's Birth-Day" also stood him in good stead; and, though he had apparently studied the "Christis Kirk" poems with considerable care and followed them in a general way, his execution of "Hallow-fair" is remarkably original.

For one thing, Fergusson introduces in it for the first time an important modification of the traditional stanza. Though he follows Ramsay and Skinner in using the simplified bobwheel, which Ramsay derived from Watson's printing of "Christis Kirk" in his *Choice Collection,* Fergusson breaks with tradition in having four instead of two rimes in the octave—that is, A B A B / C D C D / E, instead of A B A B / A B A B / C—an innovation which Burns was to adopt in "Hallowe'en" and in "The Holy Fair." For the actual incidents and circumstances in his poem, Fergusson depended entirely on his own observations. His phraseology, too, has the freshness of originality. The cunning style of "Hallow-fair" seems, indeed, to have cast a spell over later Scots poets, including Burns, who must have known the poem by heart since echoes of it crop up again and again in his work. Burns's "Holy Fair" and "Tam O'Shanter" and David Sillar's "Whisky"[16] are especially indebted to Fergusson's poem, as any careful comparison of them will show.

"Hallow-fair" is organized structurally in four main sections: the first stanza forms a brief prelude, introducing the subject and setting the scene; stanzas 2 to 8 describe the various characters at the fair and their activities: maidens seeking boy friends, "browsters" (brewers), country farmers, "chapmen billies," "cairds" (beggars), tinkers, "horse-coupers" (horse-dealers), "spae-wives" (fortune tellers), Aberdeen peddlers, recruiting sergeants, horses, and so forth; stanzas 9 to 12 deal with the City Guard, more specifically with their rough treatment of "Jock Bell," a drunkard; and the poem ends with a stanza warning all against the dire consequences of overindulgence. It will be readily seen that Fergusson's method is similar to that which he had used so effectively in "The King's Birth-Day," although in "Hallow-fair" it is more fully developed. He presents scene after scene with kaleidoscopic rapidity. Almost before the reader has time to relish one lively little sketch, he is rushed on to the next, and the next. The overall effect is cumulative; the individual pictures pile up to create a rich impression of the fair as a whole—full of life, motion, color, noise, and general confusion.

Fergusson's opening stanza is one of the most beautifully balanced in the poem, and it demonstrates his facile mastery of the difficult "Christis Kirk" stanza:

At *Hallowmas,* whan nights grow lang,
  And *starnies* shine fu' clear, — stars
Whan fock, the nippin cald to bang, — overcome
  Their winter *hap-warms* wear, — wraps
Near Edinbrough a fair there hads, — holds
  I wat there's nane whase name is, — know
For strappin dames and sturdy lads,
  And cap and stoup, mair famous — cup; drinking jug
    Than it that day.

This stanza is notable for its lightness, for the easy natural flow which Fergusson achieves in spite of the complexity of his sentence structure. The poet makes skillful use of the rime scheme to clarify his grammatical pattern: the rime of "whase name is" and "mair famous," an ingenious and playful stroke in itself, pulls together the basic structure of the sentence after a series of interrupters, and it helps to make the meaning instantly clear. It may be mentioned in passing that this stanza is similar in content to the openings of both "Christis Kirk" and "Peblis."

Stanza 2 affords examples both of Fergusson's characteristic merits and weakness as a poet. It begins with two priceless lines depicting sunrise over Edinburgh by means of a precise and suggestive image—the early morning sunlight "keeking" over the chimney-tops of the city. But the sudden shift in the middle of this stanza from the "trig made [spruce] maidens" to the "browsters rare" (brewers) is slightly disconcerting in its abruptness; for Fergusson, in his haste to plunge into the activities of the fair, tries to cram too much into this second stanza. The lines on the "browsters," taken by themselves, are, however, inimitable:

At *Hallow-fair,* whare browsters rare	
Keep gude ale on the gantries,	stands for barrels
And dinna scrimp ye o' a skair	share
O' kebbucks frae their pantries,	cheeses
Fu' saut that day.	salty

Here, the internal rime in the first line combines with the artfully placed alliteration in the second and third to give the whole passage a swinging, rollicking dash, while the sudden change of pace and pitch in the bobwheel is effected with superb artistry. Apparently, the brewers of Edinburgh during the festive season of Hallow Fair had a trick of providing free snacks of cheese prepared especially for the occasion and highly seasoned with thirst-provoking *salt* to whet the appetites of their customers. Hence the phrase "Fu' saut that day."

Fergusson's handling of the bobwheel in this and in the preceding stanza reveals, moreover, his technical versatility and his sure control of the "Christis Kirk" form. In stanza 1, the bobwheel, "Than it that day," is necessary to complete the sense of the stanza and rounds it off smoothly and effectively. In stanza 2, however, the bobwheel is not an integral part of the grammatical structure; it gives the impression of an afterthought following a a long pause, and it involves not only an abrupt slowing down of the rapid rhythm of the stanza, but also a change in pitch. The words, "Fu' saut that day," should be viewed as a kind of dramatic "aside," and should be pronounced slowly, in a low, insinuating tone of voice so as to bring out the rich flavor of the satire. The irresistibly comic effect which Fergusson achieves in this single line is, of course, only one of many brilliant imaginative touches in "Hallow-fair"; but it is worth analyzing and emphasizing as an example of Fergusson's sense of style. It is in such details that his peculiar charm and distinction as a poet lie. The line bears the unmistakable stamp of Fergusson's literary personality; he takes the reader into his confidence and comments intimately and imaginatively on the scene.

In his next few stanzas, Fergusson introduces a fascinating variety of characters, most of them disreputable. He makes good use of sound effects in this section, reproducing the peddler's crying of his wares, the shrill voice of a girl being forcibly kissed by a clumsy farmer, the screeching of the recruiting sergeant, the roaring of drunken men, and the gabbling of women and children, to create a lively impression of the general noise and tumult of the fair. He often uses direct quotation to render the sound of these voices more concrete and vivid. In stanza 3, for example, the pretended indignation of the girl, Meg, who is being chased and kissed by "country John," is suggested in her cry—

Ye silly coof! — fool
Be o' your gab mair spairin . . . — mouth

The vigorous, homely quality of Meg's expression adds greatly to the reality of the scene. In stanza 5 we hear the raucous voice of the Aberdeen peddler, as Fergusson makes expert use of the Aberdeenshire or Buchan dialect, which he had learned from the speech of his parents. The stanza is full of Aberdeenshire forms: "fa" instead of the Lowland "wha"; "guid," given the northeastern Scots pronunciation, "gweed," to rime with "need"; "protty" for "pretty"; "leem" and "teem" for "loom" and "toom" (empty). Fergusson's ability to make Sawny and, later, the guardsmen speak convincingly in their own special dialects enhances the poem's color and reality. Finally, this description of the roaring sounds of the fair comes to a climax in the admirably executed eighth stanza:

In tents the carles bend the bicker, — men; drinking bowl
An' rant an' roar like wud. — mad
Then there's sic yellowchin and din, — screaming
Wi' wives and wee-anes gablin, — children
That ane might true they were a-kin — trow
To a' the tongues at Babylon,
Confus'd that day.

After the strenuous activities of the day at the fair, the citizens of Edinburgh retired to the city to spend the evening in high-spirited conviviality. Fergusson effects this transition rapidly, yet smoothly, in stanza 9, beginning with a sly mockery of the artificial style in his first line:

When *Phoebus* ligs in *Thetis* lap, — lies
  Auld Reikie gies them shelter,
Whare cadgily they kiss the cap, — cheerfully; cup
  An' ca't round helter-skelter. — drive it
Jock Bell gaed furth to play his freaks, — tricks
  Great cause he had to rue it,
For frae a stark Lochaber aix — ax
  He gat a *clamihewit,* — severe blow
    Fu' sair that night. — sore

"Ohon!" quo' he, "I'd rather be — alas
  "By *sword* or *bagnet* stickit, — bayonet
"Than hae my crown or body wi'
  "Sic deadly weapons nicket." — such

Fergusson's skillful introduction of this comic episode, portraying the misfortunes of "Jock Bell," performs three important functions in the poem. First, it serves as a graphic and specific illustration of the boisterousness and violence of the evening's celebrations. Second, it provides a perfect opening for another attack on the City Guard, with their "stark Lochaber aixes." And third, it prepares the way for Fergusson's last stanza, with its humorous admonition on the subject of overindulgence. Jock Bell's whimsical reflection on the devastating power of "a stark Lochaber aix" in the passage cited above is a bold and amusing stroke. Here Fergusson successfully renders the ludicrous and elaborate philosophizing of a drunken man in a difficult, not to say agonizing, situation. The sadistic cruelty of the treatment which helpless Jock receives at the hands of the irresponsible City Guard is driven home with gruesome detail.

In stanza 12, Fergusson clinches his satire of the Guard, urging "good fock" to "bide yont frae this black squad," and in a final brilliant stanza he recommends moderation:

A wee soup drink dis unco weel — sip; does very
  To had the heart aboon; — hold; above
It's good as lang's a canny chiel — happy fellow
  Can stand steeve in his shoon. — steadily; shoes
But gin a birkie's owr weel sair'd — if; fellow; served

It gars him aften stammer — makes; blunder into
To *pleys* that bring him to the guard, — quarrels, broils
An' eke the *Council-chawmir,* — also; chamber
Wi' shame that day.

These lines show Fergusson in his finest vein. They have the natural rhythm and the racy colloquial diction of living speech, and yet they conform exactly to the metrical pattern. His collocation of vowel sounds in this stanza gives it a sprightly, lilting effect which contrasts pleasingly with the harsher sound patterns of the preceding stanzas. The stanza brings the poem to a happy close on a note of waggish humor, one much enhanced by the playful touch in the bobwheel—"Wi' shame that day."

With "Hallow-fair" Fergusson reached his full stature as a poet. Of all his works, "Hallow-fair" is certainly one of his most characteristic: it is filled with vigor, dash, and pulsating life, as well as with Fergusson's peculiar type of subtle humor, his inimitable "pawkiness." The imaginative brilliance of the poem never once flags or falters; there are no stylistic blunders. "Hallow-fair" is one of the few poems of Fergusson which, one feels, Burns himself would have been proud to have written.

IX "To the Tron-kirk Bell"

Two weeks after "Hallow-fair," on November 26, there appeared in *The Weekly Magazine* Fergusson's last Scots poem of 1772, "To the Tron-kirk Bell." Here Fergusson reverts to his favorite "Habbie" stanza, but he uses it this time as a vehicle for comic vituperation, or "flyting." "Flyting" was an old tradition in Scottish poetry, which had been indulged in by Dunbar, Kennedy, Lindsay, Montgomerie, and others of the fifteenth and sixteenth centuries. Fergusson's poem is clearly related to the tradition, and he follows the general method used by these masters of "flyting" in the golden age of Dunbar; but he does not seem to be specifically indebted to any of them.

Fergusson's poem is a vigorous satire on the Tron-kirk bell (and ultimately on the bailies who permit its existence) which, on account of its harsh, ear-splitting sound, he considers a public nuisance. The Tron-kirk, or, more properly, Christ's Church at the Tron, had been founded in 1637. Its notorious bell, installed in 1673, survived until 1824 when the steeple caught fire and the bell melted in the flames. Fergusson pours out his humorous vituperations on this monstrous bell, describing its nerve-wracking effects upon those citizens who live and work within its vicinity. He himself is one of these victims. He wishes he had the authority to destroy the bell, or that the town magistrates would do away with it; but, unfortunately, the magistrates live a comfortable distance away and do not have to endure its "doolfu' shock." He concludes that the bell is an engine of the Devil himself, "a cunnin snare," to keep the good folk of Edinburgh in fear and misery; and he urges that the city give the bell back to the Devil.

This poem is written with a high degree of technical skill and with great sarcastic force. Fergusson personifies the bell, and addresses himself to the bell, thus giving himself an opportunity to engage in old-fashioned personal "flyting," as the opening stanzas reveals:

Wanwordy, crazy, dinsome thing,	worthless
As e'er was fram'd to jow or ring,	toll
What gar'd them sic in steeple hing	made; such; hang
They ken themsel',	
But weel wat I they coudna bring	know
War sounds frae hell.	worse

This stanza sets the zestful mood of the whole poem. In his next stanzas Fergusson develops this comic personification of the bell. He asks, "What de'il are ye?" and concludes, with mock gravity, "Your neither kin to pat nor pan." He compares the bell's "noisy tongue" with that of a "scaulding wife"; and, in the tail-lines of stanzas 3 and 4, he uses onomatopoeic words—"bang," "twang," "thole," "knoll"—to suggest the jarring sound it produces. In stanza 5, the note of violent personal animosity against the bell rises to a vigorous climax:

O! war I provost o' the town,	were; mayor
I swear by a' the pow'rs aboon,	above
I'd bring ye wi' a reesle down;	clatter
Nor shud you think	
(Sae sair I'd crack and clour your crown)	batter
Again to clink.	

The poet's violent threat in the parenthetical fifth line above reinforces the ludicrous personification of the bell, and it evokes an amusing visual image of Fergusson frantically beating it into insensibility, once he has gotten his hands on it. In stanzas 7 and 8, Fergusson describes a dream in which he sees "Auld Nick" gloating over his "dautit [pet] bell," and in his final stanza the poet calls upon the magistrates to return the diabolical instrument to its rightful owner:

But far frae thee the *bailies* dwell,	magistrates
Or they wud scunner at your knell,	shudder
Gie the *foul thief* his riven bell,	the devil
And than, I trow,	
The by-word hads, "the de'il himsel'	holds
"Has got his due."	

"To the Tron-kirk Bell" requires less elucidation and comment than most of Fergusson's Scots poems. It is sufficient unto itself as an original, highly amusing piece of old-fashioned personal "flyting" applied to an inanimate object. It has many touches of Fergusson's typically tricksy humor, his bold and ingenious imagination, and his facile, accomplished technique. The poem, consistently good in its execution, represents one of Fergusson's most original and witty commentaries on life and manners in Old Edinburgh.

X *The Year 1772*

Looking back over Fergusson's Scots poems of 1772, one is struck by the remarkable diversity they show within a fairly limited range, and by their originality. During this, his first year of substantial production as a vernacular poet, Fergusson was apparently trying his hand at a variety of traditional Scots genres: the elegy in the "Habbie" stanza, the familiar epistle, the Scottish pastoral, the "Christis Krik" genre, and the "flyting" poem. In most of these types, he was immediately successful; and in two of them, the Scottish pastoral and the "Christis Kirk" genre, he introduced important changes. The success he achieved in these poems is all the more astonishing when we consider his youthfulness—he had just turned twenty-two in September of 1772—and the fact that most of these poems were his first known attempts in the particular genres. Yet he handles these traditional forms with an ease that suggests long experience.

In addition to his skillful writings in these historic genres, Fergusson, in "The Daft-Days," "The King's Birth-Day," "Caller Oysters," and "Braid Claith," developed a new type of Scottish poem which was to have a powerful influence on Burns—the poem of homely and realistic social description, with satiric tendencies, in the "Habbie" stanza. The historical importance of his brilliant extension of the "Habbie" tradition in this direction can scarcely be overemphasized.

Finally, these poems of 1772 show clear evidence of Fergusson's steady, amazingly rapid development as a poet. There is a constant and decided improvement, both in general technique and in imaginative powers. The early poems—"The Daft-Days," "Elegy on Scots Music," "The King's Birth-Day," and "Caller Oysters" are all marred to some extent by weaknesses which gradually disappear in the later pieces. "Braid Claith," "An Eclogue," "Hallow-fair," and "To the Tron-kirk Bell" reveal a consistent ripeness and mastery of technique and a firmness of structure which are not present in earlier works. Furthermore, Fergusson's imaginative daring, his willingness to experiment with new forms and devices, is on the increase toward the end of 1772, as comparison of two poems on similar themes—"The Daft-Days" and "Hallow-fair"—will show. Also, the ease and versatility with which he handles his verse forms have clearly improved; and in the later poems, especially in "Braid Claith," "An Eclogue," and "Hallow-fair," he shows a new and delightful ability to depict characters in a few graphic strokes—an ability which does not appear at all in the earlier poems.

Another significant fact emerges from a survey of Fergusson's Scots poems of 1772: six out of the nine poems that can be accurately dated belong to the last third of the year. After producing only three Scots poems in nearly eight months, Fergusson, starting with "Caller Oysters" on August 29, suddenly began to turn them out in rapid succession. This marked upsurge in creative activity means that Fergusson had finally discovered himself. Probably the glowing epistle of J. S. helped to spur him on. At any rate, he had found the work he was destined to do, and he set to it with a will.

CHAPTER 4

Scots Poems of 1773:
"Caller Water" to "Leith Races"

> O Fergusson! thy glorious parts
> Ill suited law's dry, musty arts!
> My curse upon your whunstane hearts;
>   Ye E'nbrugh gentry!
> The tythe o' what ye waste at cartes
>   Wad stow'd his pantry!
>
> BURNS

IN 1773 Fergusson produced some twenty-one Scots poems, many of them of first-rate importance. It was by far his greatest and most prolific year, during which he brought forth one little masterpiece after another at an average of one every three weeks. The fertility and speed of Fergusson's composition during this period are remarkable when we consider that he was also turning out poems in English with almost equal frequency, and that he remained at his full-time clerical position in the Commissary Office.

I "Caller Water"

Fergusson published no Scots poetry whatsoever during the last month of 1772, probably because he was busy preparing his collection of *Poems* for the press. But on January 21, 1773, a new Scots poem, "Caller Water" (cold water), appeared in Ruddiman's *Weekly Magazine* over his signature, and was reprinted on February 26 in *The Perth Magazine*.[1] This clever poem, in fifteen "Habbie" stanzas, praises the health-giving, beautifying qualities of clear cold water, as contrasted, ironically, with the enfeebling effects of alcoholic liquors. The work has historical interest as having suggested the whole concept of Burn's "Scotch Drink" as well as that of David Sillar's "Whisky." [2] Moreover, some of Fergusson's actual phrasing in "Caller Water" seems to have stuck in Burn's mind, cropping up in the opening lines of "Scotch Drink" ("Let other poets raise a frácas / 'Bout vines, an' wines, an' drucken Bacchus" from Fergusson's stanza 4: "The fuddlin' Bardies now-a-days / Rin *maukin*-mad in Bacchus' praise"), and again in a charming line in the fifteenth stanza of "Address to the Deil" ("Lang syne in Eden's bonie yard," echoing Fergusson's opening stanza: "The bonny yeard of antient Eden").

In his first three stanzas, Fergusson introduces his theme with a delightfully humanized and humorous sketch of Adam's life in the garden of Eden:

Whan father *Adie* first pat spade in	put
The bonny yeard of antient Eden,	garden
His amry had nae liquor laid in	cupboard
To fire his mou',	mouth
Nor did he thole his wife's upbraidin'	endure
For being fou.	drunk

The poet is here whimsically interpreting Adam's existence in terms of "spade," "amry," "liquor," and scolding wife—that is, in terms of eighteenth-century Scottish peasant life. The comparison is amusing in itself, and it is greatly enhanced by Fergusson's familiar treatment of the patriarch. With the typical Scottish fondness for nick-names, he calls Adam "Adie" and, in stanza 2, "our gutcher" (grandfather). Both expressions, strongly colloquial and intimate in flavor, are skillfully chosen to build up a comfortable and familiar impression of Adam, as though he were an old-fashioned Midlothian farmer.

The contrast between Adam's simple, wholesome life, as reflected in his healthy enjoyment of "caller water," and the intense social life of modern Edinburgh, as revealed in its heavy drinking, is developed in the next stanzas and brought to a comic culmination in the lines:

His bairns a' before the flood	children
Had langer tack o' flesh and blood,	lease
And on mair pithy shanks they stood	sturdy
Than *Noah's* line,	
Wha still hae been a feckless brood	feeble
Wi' drinking wine.	

This stanza strikes a note of droll exaggeration sustained throughout the poem. The last line, "Wi' drinking wine," leads smoothly into the next stanza in which Fergusson makes fun of the modern poetic fashion of praising strong drink—a fashion, incidentally, which he himself followed in other poems. It is significant that Fergusson's vernacular idiom in this stanza, as in other scattered phrases in "Caller Water," is strong and supple enough to incorporate references to Classical mythology and poetry successfully into its texture.[3]

Fergusson's second group of stanzas (6-9), on the medicinal values of water, is notable for its derisive scorn of doctors with their elaborate drugs and superfluous Latin jargon, a note which he had already sounded in "Caller Oysters." His own recommendation, in stanzas 8 and 9, of "caller water" as a sovereign cure for rheumatism, colic, heart-burn, "or any inward pain," is ludicrously exaggerated—

'Twill mak you souple, swack and young,   limber
    Withouten drugs.

Fergusson's lack of confidence in medical men probably had something to do with his own experience, threatened as he was by ill health and haunted by the fear of it.

At this point, the poem takes a surprising turn as Fergusson, through a smooth transition (stanzas 10 and 11) from the health-giving to the beautifying qualities of water, transforms the latter part of "Caller Water" into a eulogy on Auld Reekie's sparkling lasses:

Wer't na for it the bonny lasses
Would glowr nae mair in keeking glasses . . .   looking-glasses
. . . .
The fairest then might die a maid,
And Cupid quit his shooting trade . . .

Fergusson's happy choice of the phrase "shooting trade," which recalls the barber's "scrapin wark" in "Braid Claith," helps to create the slyly humorous quality of style which is a prominent characteristic of the poem as a whole. Stanza 13 contains a satiric, local allusion which must have delighted his contemporaries:

What makes Auld Reikie's dames sae fair,	
It canna be the halesome air,	wholesome
But *caller burn* beyond compare,	fresh brook (water)
The best of ony,	
That gars them a' sic graces skair,	makes; such; share
And blink sae bonny.	look

Edinburgh was notorious in Fergusson's day for its inefficient sewage disposal and, consequently, for the foul smells which pervaded its narrow wynds and closes. The point of Fergusson's wry comment, "It canna be the halesome air," must have been pungently obvious to his fellow citizens.

The last two stanzas are the weakest in the poem. In them Fergusson's strong, humorous style fades out and he lapses gradually into the pretty conventionality of the pastoral tradition. Stanza 14 is further weakened by what seems to be a fault in grammar in the line, "And water clear as chrystal spring," in which a verb is required in place of the noun, "spring." [4] In all probability, "spring" is a printer's error for some verb—"bring," perhaps, or "fling." Since "Caller Water" was not reprinted in the *Poems* of 1773, Fergusson had no opportunity to revise his text. Even with the error corrected, however, the stanza is weak. And the final stanza, though neatly turned and appropriately light and graceful in tone, is nevertheless disappointing, with its hackneyed phrases—"pursue the way," "beauties glance like *May*," and "the goddess of the vocal Spray"—marring the artistic integrity of an otherwise fine poem.

It is worthwhile to speculate on the reason that Fergusson frequently ends vernacular poems on a strongly conventional note. Occasionally, as we have seen in the "Elegy on Scots Music" and in "The King's Birth-Day," he introduces such passages for purposes of irony. But, more often, they seem to be conscious and deliberate efforts to dress up his poems in the conventional poetic idiom. His own fresh and daring style struggles against the genteel tradition; yet he wants people to take him seriously as a poet. And he is afraid they will not do so if his work differs too radically from what eighteenth-century readers had come to expect and accept as poetry. Therefore, these bits of "poetic diction" and conventional imagery in the last lines of several good Scots poems attempt to dignify them, to relate them to the accepted norms of poetic style, and to bring them back, as it were, into the tradition.

II "Plainstanes and Causey"

Fergusson's next Scots poem, the "Mutual Complaint of Plainstanes and Causey, In Their Mother-tongue," was published in *The Weekly Magazine* on March 4, six weeks after "Caller Water." It is a humorous argument, or "flyting," in tetrameter couplets between two imaginary characters, the "plainstanes" (sidewalks) and "causey" (street or roadway) of the High Street in Edinburgh. During the argument, each complains to the other of the rough traffic he has to bear.

"Plainstanes and Causey" is obviously related, in its method, to the ancient Scottish "flyting" tradition, but with a difference. In the old "flyting" poems, such as constitute the celebrated exchange between Dunbar and Kennedy, the poet gives only one side of the argument, expressing his own personal point of view; but in "Plainstanes and Causey," Fergusson gives both sides of the argument between two imaginary characters of his own creation. Fergusson is here, in fact, combining two traditions: the old Scots "flyting" genre (with its personal vituperation) and the "eclogue" genre (with its duologue form) as he found it in eighteenth-century English and Scottish pastoral eclogues. As we have seen, he had already tried his hand at the "flyting" poem in "To the Tron-kirk Bell," and at the pastoral eclogue in "An Eclogue" and in "Eclogue on Wilkie." In "Plainstanes and Causey," he combines these traditions, and in so doing creates a new poetic form, which might be called the "flyting eclogue," and which he passed on to Burns. "Plainstanes and Causey" is, moreover, brilliantly original in its subject and in its fanciful use of inanimate objects as characters, and is acknowledged by all commentators to have been the model for Burns's "The Brigs of Ayr." In method and in general humorous tone, "The Twa Dogs" is also related to Fergusson's poem.

In connection with "The Brigs of Ayr," it is worth noting that "Plainstanes and Causey" is one of Fergusson's poems which has suffered from a grossly prejudiced, uncritical comparison with Burns. Most of the writers on Fergusson and Burns, starting with the preconception that Burns *always* improved upon his models, have failed to see these two poems in a clear and unbiased light; and, as a result, they have almost automatically judged "The Brigs of Ayr" as infinitely superior.[5] Yet a careful reading of both works will show that, in respect to artistic integrity at least, "Plainstanes and Causey" is a better poem than "The Brigs of Ayr." Burns's poem is lacking in fundamental unity: it opens with a rather pompous dedicatory introduction in the English neo-Classical style which gradually fades out as the poem progresses into the central section, the "flyting" proper, which is rendered in vigorous and racy vernacular. After the "flyting" between the "twa brigs" ends, Burns introduces his absurdly incongruous "vision" of the "Genius of the River" with attendant spirits, and he closes his poem with a feeble throng of neo-Classical abstractions. The only part of the poem which has real and substantial merit is the central portion, the duologue itself—the section in which Burns leans most heavily on Fergusson. Though Burns's expression here is occasionally more vigorous and brilliant than Fergusson's, Fergusson's poem has the advantage of more vivid human interest, presenting lively and specific glimpses of Edinburgh life and characters.

"Plainstanes and Causey" begins with a charming introductory passage in which Fergusson tells how a quick-witted "cadie" or messenger boy, wandering in the street late at night, accidentally overheard the fantastic conversation between "plainstanes" and "causey" and reported it to the poet early next morning. Burns, we may note, employs a similar method of introducing the duologue in his "Brigs of Ayr"; in it the poet, during a midnight stroll by the river, overhears the bridges arguing back and forth. Fergusson's passage opens with a magnificent bit of comic ambiguity:

Since *Merlin* laid Auld Reikie's causey,	
And made her o' his wark right saucy,	proud
The spacious *street* and *plainstanes*	
Were never kend to crack but anes . . .	talk; once

The ambiguity here lies in the use of the verb "crack," which in Scots has two meanings: "to split," as in standard English, or, more colloquially, "to converse." The unsuspecting reader of these lines naturally assumes that Fergusson is using the word in its literal sense, "to split," since he is speaking of inanimate paving stones which, as everyone knows, do have an unfortunate tendency to "crack." Four lines later, however, the poem takes a sudden twist which reveals the true situation in a flash:

Of Highland sentries nane were waukin,	awake
To hear thir cronies glibbly taukin . . .	these

Fergusson springs his surprise on the reader soon after his use of the ambiguous verb "crack," so that, when the reader makes the startling discovery that the sidewalk and street are "taukin," his mind jumps back to the word "crack" four lines above, the real significance of which has now become apparent. The ingenious deception of the opening lines dawns upon the delighted reader in a flash. The brilliance of the thing is not only pleasing in itself; it also sets the mood of imaginative nonsense and forces the reader to make a conscious mental adjustment which enables him to accept the fantastic conversation that follows.

The very neatly constructed duologue begins on a relatively subdued note of disgruntled complaint, gradually rises to a climax of vehement dispute in the middle, and then in the conclusion slowly subsides into the harmonious mood of compromise. It opens with Plainstane's first speech in which Fergusson begins to reveal the dominant traits of that sensitive individual. Plainstanes is, of course, a clearly recognizable human type; and Fergusson sketches his character, or rather makes him reveal his own character, with remarkable precision. Plainstanes is an effeminate fop, with strong tendencies toward hypochrondria, amorous flirtation, and snobbishness. He resents the intrusion upon his aristocratic pavement of such vulgar tradesmen as "mealy bakers," "hair-kaimers" (barbers), and "crieshy gezymakers" (greasy wig-makers), who clutter up the sidewalk which rightfully belongs to the "beaux" and "ladies." The presence of these tradesmen forces the ladies to wear hats and veils, thus inhibiting sidewalk flirtations and depriving Plainstanes of a vicarious diversion. He complains finally and most bitterly of the Highland chairmen:

Speak, was I made to dree the laidin	endure; load
Of Gallic chairman heavy treadin,	Gaelic
Wha in my tender buke bore holes	body
Wi' waefu' tackets i' the soals	woeful nails

O' broags, whilk on my body tramp,   heavy shoes; which
And wound like death at ilka clamp.

Plainstanes' hypersensitivity to pain and discomfort is thus amusingly revealed.

The rough-and-ready Causey scoffs at this sort of effeminacy and self-pity:

  Weil crackit friend—It aft hads true,   spoken; holds
Wi' naething fock make maist ado . . .   most

The heavy irony of Causey's first words, "Weil crackit friend," deftly suggests his shrewd sense of humor, while the rest of his speech shows his robust, practical outlook on life. His manner of speaking, it will be noticed, is more vigorous, direct, brief and to the point than that of the long-winded and fastidious Plainstanes, whose second speech, beginning ludicrously with the words, "Had sae [hold so], and lat me get a word in," is the lengthiest in the poem. The passage which follows, in which Plainstanes contrasts Causey's rugged construction, made from "whin-stanes, howkit frae the craigs" (hard rocks, dug from the crags), with his own "weak and feckless" body, is highly amusing and beautifully executed. His next remarks are even funnier. Plainstanes describes, with evident relish, his experience with "patens" (pattens), the wooden "lifts" worn by Edinburgh ladies in wet weather:

I grant, indeed, that, now and than,   then
Yield to a *paten's* pith I maun;   force; must
But patens, tho' they're aften plenty,
Are ay laid down wi' feet fou tenty,   careful
And stroaks frae ladies, tho' they're teazing,
I freely maun avow are pleasing.

This endowing of the foppish Plainstanes with a timid sort of erotic personality is one of the boldest imaginative strokes in the poem, and one of the most laughable. Plainstanes obviously fancies himself as a ladies' man, with a protective instinct which appears rather ridiculous in view of his admittedly "weak and feckless" nature:

But gin I guess aright, my trade is   if
To fend frae skaith the bonny ladies . . .   harm

He concludes his speech with an absurd attempt to browbeat Causey: he threatens to take his case to law—just the kind of threat that we might expect such a person to make.

Causey reacts to this threat with characteristic vigor, as he blurts out contemptuously—

I dinna care a single jot,	
Tho' summon'd by a shelly-coat,	sheriff's officer
Sae leally I'll propone defences,	truly, vigorously
As get ye flung for my expences . . .	baffled, defeated

In the first place, Causey maintains that his hardships are more severe, even making allowances for his stronger constitution, since he has to bear enormous loads which would "fret the hardest stane"—namely, the burden of the Luckenbooths and the Guard-house ("A lumbersome and stinkin bigging, / That rides the sairest on my rigging"), buildings which stood in the middle of the High Street.

Causey's reference, in this speech, to "*Charlie's Statue*" and "*Exchange*" may have something to do with the original inspiration of the entire poem. For centuries the merchants and lawyers of Edinburgh had been accustomed to gathering to discuss business matters every afternoon on the open street near the Mercat Cross. About the time of the removal of the Cross in 1756, the city authorities had "plainstanes" laid in these two places—at the "Royal Exchange" and around the statue of Charles II in Parliament Square—for the convenience of the businessmen. The merchants and lawyers, however, completely ignored these arrangements and continued to meet at their old haunt on the open "causey" near the site of the Cross. Their stubborn preference gave rise to innumerable local jokes and humorous allusions in Fergusson's time, and these may very well have suggested to him the idea of writing a poem about the dispute between "plainstanes" and "causey." However this may be, Causey closes his short but trenchant speech by proposing a compromise: he will agree to carry the "trades-fock and country Johnies," so long as Plainstanes takes care of his "beaux and macaronies." Plainstanes is quick to accept, and the dispute is resolved in the final speeches.

In "Plainstanes and Causey" Fergusson reverted to the tetrameter couplet, that old and popular Scottish verse form which he had used only once before, in his earliest known poem, the translation from Horace. His handling of the couplet is generally competent and sometimes very effective, but he is not yet completely at home in this form. One misses in this work the ease and fluency which Fergusson had shown in the "Habbie" and "Christis Kirk" stanzas, the technical brilliance of such poems as "Braid Claith," "Hallow-fair," and "To the Tron-kirk Bell." That the poem has great appeal, however, cannot be denied. It is a delightful fantasy, one of Fergusson's most imaginative efforts. Its distinctive charm lies in the originality of the initial idea, in the superb ingenuity of its execution, and in its abiding human interest. "Plainstanes and Causey" is packed with human appeal and shrewd characterization. Its interest lies not only in the wonderfully vivid characters of the speakers themselves, but also in the intimate glimpses of the Edinburgh manners they describe. The character sketch of Plainstanes, for fullness of humorous detail and subtle suggestiveness, is perhaps the best in all Fergusson's work. The poem is, indeed, infused wih an irresistibly comic view of the life it portrays in dramatic and artistic form. For these reasons, "Plainstanes and Causey" ranks high among Fergusson's poems, though it is not one of his very best.

III "The Rising of the Session"

In his next Scots poem, "The Rising of the Session," Fergusson went back to his favorite "Habbie" stanza. The poem appeared in *The Weekly Magazine* on March 18, just two weeks after "Plainstanes and Causey," and it is one of the very few poems dated as to time of composition by Fergusson himself. It bears the date, "*Auld Reikie, March* 15, 1773," indicating that Fergusson finished the poem just three days before it was published by Ruddiman. Obviously another occasional piece, this poem was written to commemorate the ending of the winter term of the Court of Session, the supreme Scottish judicial body, which adjourned in March. It describes, with strong satirical touches, the general exodus of lawyers from Edinburgh to the country at the end of the session, and the effects of this exodus on various classes in the city, especially on the tavern-keepers. Though the poem is clearly organized in two main sections—the first half (stanzas 1-7) dealing with the happy fortunes of those who leave town at the end of the session; the second, with the harder fate of those who remain behind—within these divisions "The Rising of the Session" is rather miscellaneous in content and, it must be admitted, somewhat loose in structure, lacking the unifying mood of other social descriptive pieces, such as "The Daft-Days," "The King's Birth-Day," or "Hallow-fair."

In the details of its composition, however, "The Rising of the Session" is a competent and skillful poem. It opens with an amusing imitation of the style of official proclamations:

To a' men living be it kend,	
The SESSION now is at an end:	
Writers, your finger-nebbs unbend,	finger-ends
And quatt the pen,	quit
Till *Time* wi' lyart pow shall send	hoary head
Blythe June again.	

The reference here to "finger-nebbs" is typical of the particularity of Fergusson's style, of the vivid and well-chosen details with which his poems are usually enriched. He was himself only too well acquainted with writer's cramp, and no doubt the unbending of "finger-nebbs" occurred to him as a fitting symbol of emancipation from drudgery. At any rate, after a mischievous satiric thrust at the lawyers in stanza 3, Fergusson contrasts the fortunes of rich and poor in two stanzas which are worth quoting in full for the sake of the attitude they reveal:

Blythe they may be wha wanton play	
In *fortune's* bonny blinkin ray,	
Fu' weel can they ding dool away	drive sorrow
Wi' comrades couthy,	sociable
And never dree a hungert day,	endure; hungry
Or e'ening drouthy.	thirsty
Ohon the day for him that's laid,	alas
In dowie *poortith's* caldrife shade,	sad poverty's chilly
Ablins owr honest for his trade,	perhaps
He racks his wits,	
How he may get his buick weel clad,	body
And fill his guts.	

Fergusson's vision of ideal riches is indeed a modest one: it consists merely of having plenty to eat, plenty to drink, decent clothes, and leisure to enjoy himself with "comrades couthy."

These simple comforts of life Fergusson longed for; but, in spite of his talent, he was destined never to possess them. The passage is filled with the poignancy of his desire, with the tragedy of a gifted, happy spirit who found himself trapped in "dowie *poortith's* caldrife shade." Perhaps there is even a touch of bitterness in the line, "Ablins owr honest for his trade," an implied indictment of the legal "trade" in which a man who was "owr honest" had little chance for advancement.

In the latter part of the poem, Fergusson's fine comic observation shows to better advantage, especially in his lively portraits of tavern life during the "vacance time." Robin Gibb and Peter Williamson both kept taverns in the "Outer House," as the old Parliament Hall of Edinburgh was called, where the Court of Session was held; and, therefore, both come in for whimsical treatment at Fergusson's hands. The tenth stanza, on Robin Gibb, is one of the highlights of the poem:

Nae body takes a morning dribb	drop
O' *Holland gin* frae *Robin Gibb;*	
And tho' a dram to Rob's mair sib	akin
Than is his wife,	
He maun take time to daut his *Rib*	pet, fondle; wife
Till siller's rife.	silver, money

Fergusson's condensation and economy of expression are remarkable in these lines. He manages to suggest the whole character of the man in a single bold satiric stroke, vaguely reminiscent of Chaucer's method in the Prologue to the *Canterbury Tales.* The picture of Rob taking time off from his favorite "drams" to "daut his *Rib*" during the slack season is priceless, and it is much enhanced by Fergusson's use of the strongly vernacular word "sib," and the brilliantly imaginative "*Rib,*" both of which are calculated to strike exactly the right note of genial humor. Fergusson's final comic plea for patience on the part of the tavern-keepers is finely executed:

Ye change-house keepers never grumble,	
Tho' you a while your bickers whumble . . .	drinking-cups turn upside down
You needna grudge to draw your breath	
For little mair than haf a reath,	quarter of a year
Than, gin we a' be spar'd frae death,	if

We'll gladly prie	taste
Fresh noggans o' your reaming graith	frothing goods
Wi' blythsome glee.	

In these bright and gently satiric lines, Fergusson rounds off his poem on a note of sunny laughter.

All in all, however, "The Rising of the Session," though it contains some excellent passages, gives the impression of a hastily written occasional piece. Fergusson's usually careful craftsmanship is not very apparent here. The poem is loose in its structure; though many of the individual parts are well done in themselves, they do not work together to create a single unified effect. In hurriedly writing the poem, Fergusson allowed his descriptive method to get out of control; as a result, the poem leaves a rather confused impression. In spite of several delightful and characteristic touches, "The Rising of the Session" cannot, on the whole, be regarded as one of Fergusson's better Scots poems.

IV "Ode to the Bee"

Fergusson's next vernacular work, the "Ode to the Bee," represents for him an entirely new departure. It was published in *The Weekly Magazine* on April 29, and, like "The Rising of the Session," was dated by the author: "*Broomhouse, East-Lothian, April* 26, 1773," three days before its publication. The East Lothian address suggests that the poem was written during one of Fergusson's week-end jaunts into the countryside around Edinburgh. The "Ode to the Bee," curiously enough, was not included in the 1779 edition of Fergusson, but was reprinted for the first time in Ruddiman's second edition of 1782.[6]

In this ode Fergusson was experimenting with an entirely new type of poem, one peculiarly unsuited to his special talents. It belongs to the well-established eighteenth-century English tradition of pastoral meditative poetry, a tradition which goes back to "L'Allegro" and "Il Penseroso" of Milton and which exerted tremendous influence upon James Thomson's *Seasons* and Edward Young's *Night Thoughts*. In this type of poetry the the philosophic, didactic poet finds "sermons in stones"; he describes some aspect of nature, and then draws from it some moral lesson for the guidance of man. Fergusson's ode falls squarely into this contemplative tradition, and it is excessively imitative both in its commonplace theme and method and, to a lesser extent, in phraseology. It is worth mentioning in passing that Fergusson, in this poem and in his later "Ode to the Gowdspink," passed on the genre to Burns, whose "To a Mountain Daisy," for example, is based on precisely the same method: that of drawing general moral lessons from the contemplation of a specific object in nature.

The style of the "Ode to the Bee" is a curious hybrid, in which elements of three different styles can be clearly distinguished: Fergusson's pure Scots, Ramsay's Scoto-English pastoral style, and the stereotyped phraseology of English neo-Classical nature poetry. In the first part of the ode (lines 1-22) the two latter styles predominate. Such phrases as "tune your canty reeds" and "gowany meads," for example, are strongly reminiscent of Ramsay's pastorals. The influence of the neo-Classical manner reveals itself even more clearly in "voice delights the spring," "disclose their sweets," "skim on wanton wing," and "fairy haunts of spring." Though these hackneyed expressions take on a degree of freshness when found in the vernacular context, they weaken the poem and make it appear a conventional exercise, lacking in sincere poetic feeling. In the last four couplets of his opening section, however, Fergusson does somewhat better:

Whan fields ha'e got their dewy gift,	
And dawnin breaks upo' the lift,	sky
Then gang ye're wa's thro' *hight* and *how,*	go; ways; hollow
Seek caller *haugh* or sunny *know,*	cool riverside; knoll
Or ivy'd *craig* or *burnbank brae,*	brookside slope
Whare industry shall bid ye gae,	go
For hiney or for waxen store,	honey
To ding sad poortith frae your door.	drive; poverty

These lines, in spite of "dewy gift" and "waxen store," convey a more genuinely lyrical feeling; and the last line, "To ding sad poortith frae your door," makes for a smooth transition to the next section (lines 23-46) on man's improvidence. The central portion of the ode is an unhappy mixture of fairly effective vernacular description and of banal moralizing. The passage contains such woodenly conventional couplets as—

Then feeble man, be wise, take tent — heed
How industry can fetch content . . .

Yet this is followed by several delicate and smoothly turned lines on the bee's activities, ending—

Or whan on open bent they're seen, — field
On *hether-bell* or *thristle* green; — thistle
The hiney's still as sweet that flows — honey
Frae thristle cald or kendling rose. — kindling

At this point, however, the poem sinks again into trite philosophizing and artificial diction which continues through the third section of the poem (lines 47-58) in which Fergusson imagines himself living a quiet life in the country, affording protection to the bees around his "cell." The final verse paragraph, however, in which he likens his poetic muse to the bee, is worth noticing as evidence that Fergusson had by this time come to look upon himself as a poet in a higher sense, rather than as a part-time versifier:

Like thee, by fancy wing'd, the Muse
Scuds ear' and heartsome o'er the dews, — skims early
Fu' vogie, and fu' blyth to crap — glad; crop
The winsome flow'rs frae Nature's lap,
Twining her living garlands there,
That lyart time can ne'er impair. — hoary

In these lines the poem rises above the hackneyed treatment of the rest. Though Fergusson's expression here is by no means inspired, the feeling he expresses rings true; the exalted conception of his muse contrasts significantly with the earlier attitude revealed in the "Answer to J. S.," in which he speaks of his "knack, / To gar auld-warld wordies clack / In hamespun rhime."

It was probably Fergusson's new and more dignified attitude toward himself as a poet which led to his artistic failure in the "Ode to the Bee." For over a year he had been turning out poetry which had delighted readers all over Scotland with its lively realism tinged with sharp irony and satire. It had won him fame as a new national poet. Perhaps at this point Fergusson became ambitious to dignify his position, to prove to himself and to the public that he was capable of handling sober and elevated themes. Accordingly, he attempts this serious, didactic poem—and fails. He fails because he chose to write in a genre unsuited to his special abilities: his theme offers little opportunity for the rich, vivid observation of men and manners at which Fergusson excelled. Thus, a large portion of his poem resolves itself into dull generalities and worn-out formulas, although some passages do show a genuine and joyous feeling for nature and, occasionally, a degree of minute, realistic treatment of it which are unusual for the time and give to these passages a certain freshness.

By and large, however, the ode lacks distinction because Fergusson, in attempting this genre for the first time, did not have sufficient confidence to express himself naturally in his own individual style but slipped back into an imitation of the conventional style of his models. Significantly enough, the "Ode to the Bee" was one of Fergusson's Scots poems most admired by the early commentators. David Irving, for example, calls it a fine specimen of Scottish lyric poetry, "a due intermixture of picturesque description and well-turned moral reflection." [7] Such comments are typical of the vitiated taste of an age which worshipped shallow prettiness and heavy-handed didacticism in poetry. The "Ode to the Bee" came in for special praise simply because, of all Fergusson's vernacular poems, it comes closest to the genteel tradition in eighteenth-century Scots poetry.

V "The Farmer's Ingle"

Fergusson's next Scots poem, "The Farmer's Ingle," represents a second and far more successful attempt to dignify his position and to extend his range as a poet. Published in *The Weekly Magazine* on May 13 and reprinted in *The Perth Magazine* (IV, 242-45) on May 21, this poem is written in a modified form of the Spenserian stanza; and it describes an evening's activities around the fireside of a typical Scottish farmer.

"The Farmer's Ingle" has generally been considered Fergusson's masterpiece, and it has consequently received more attention from critics than any other of his works. Certainly, it is one of his most ambitious and most original poems. The germinal idea for "The Farmer's Ingle" may have come from Virgil's *Bucolics,* three lines of which Fergusson takes as the motto for his poem; but more likely it was suggested by some of the descriptive passages in Ramsay's *The Gentle Shepherd,* especially by Peggy's speech beginning "At Even, when he comes weary frae the Hill" in Act I, Scene 2, where she envisions how she will take care of her husband when he comes home at night. On the whole, however, "The Farmer's Ingle" seems to be almost entirely original, a new departure in Scottish poetry, both in subject matter and treatment. It is, as James Logie Robertson says,[8] the first Scottish poem to deal "seriously, directly, and exclusively" with the simple life of the farmer and his family.

Its verse form, too, is unusual: Fergusson here employs the Spenserian stanza for the first time in Scottish poetry. He modifies the stanza—which, incidentally, he picked up from English eighteenth-century Spenserianism, perhaps from Beattie's "Minstrel," or Thomson's "Castle of Indolence," but most probably from Shenstone's "Schoolmistress"—by introducing an extra rime (A B A B, C D C D, D instead of A B A B, B C B C, C). This variation, it will be noted, is very similar to the change which Fergusson made in the "Christis Kirk" stanza, in which he added extra rimes for greater flexibility. Fergusson deviates further from the Spenserian pattern in retaining the pentameter in his ninth lines, except in stanzas 4, 7, and 13, where he employs the usual Alexandrine.

"The Farmer's Ingle" has been universally recognized as the model for Burns's "Cotter's Saturday Night." The relationships between the two poems in subject, thematic development, and verse form are, indeed, too obvious to require detailed comment. But in almost all respects Fergusson's poem is by far the better; and it is time that the inferiority of "The Cotter's Saturday Night" be more generally recognized by modern students of Scottish poetry—as David Daiches has so clearly demonstrated in his excellent study of the poem.[9] Burns's poem has, of course, been long admired, chiefly for its sentimental nonsense and insincere moralizing. Nineteenth-century critics unanimously prefer it to the less pretentious, but more realistic and genuinely artistic "Farmer's Ingle." Modern critics have less excuse for this distorted judgment; yet it persists, as the commentaries of Sir George Douglas,[10] Frank Beaumont,[11] and others show. Any thorough and objective analysis of the two poems, however, must lead to the conclusion that "The Cotter's Saturday Night" is one of the few poems in which Burns failed to surpass, or even to equal, his model.

"The Farmer's Ingle" is simply but effectively organized in thirteen stanzas, describing the routine events of the evening as they happen. In essence, the poem is a series of lively little pictures of country life, intimately and sympathetically drawn to reveal the goodness, simplicity, and quiet beauty of that life rather than its harsher aspects. It is filled with a gentle idealism and a moving, unostentatious patriotism; but the idealism is not expressed, as it so often is in "The Cotter's Saturday Night," through empty generalization; it is expressed through Fergusson's choice of realistic detail faithfully presented and suffused with a glow of tenderness and sympathetic humanity.

The first stanza of "The Farmer's Ingle" illustrates both the merits and weaknesses of the poem:

When gloming grey out o'er the welkin keeks,	twilight; looks
When *Batie* ca's his owsen to the byre,	drives; cowhouse
When *Thrasher John*, sair dung, his barn-door	tired
steeks,	shuts
And lusty lasses at the dighting tire:	winnowing
What bangs fu' leal the e'enings coming cauld,	defeats; thoroughly
And gars snaw-tapit winter freeze in vain;	makes snow-topped
Gars dowie mortals look baith blyth and bauld,	sad; both; bold
Nor fley'd wi' a' the poortith o' the plain;	frightened;
Begin, my Muse, and chant in hamely strain.	poverty

In the first four lines (which, incidentally, are reminiscent of the opening of Gray's "Elegy" in tone and of the first lines of Shakespeare's famous song from *Love's Labor's Lost*, "When icicles hang by the wall," both in construction and in the type of realistic, highly specific detail used), Fergusson gives us brief but vivid glimpses of the various farm workers at the end of a long, weary day. The slow rhythm and long vowel sounds in these lines reinforce the feeling of weariness as the laborers plod home at dusk. Burns successfully achieves the same effect in the second stanza of his "Cotter's Saturday Night." Fergusson's next five lines, in comparison with the first part of his opening stanza, are not so effective, for they contain an involved grammatical inversion which smacks of an artificiality hardly appropriate to a "hamely strain." The entire stanza is, in fact, a single sentence with the main verbs "begin" and "chant" in the last line. "What" in line 5 is the object of the verb "chant" in line 9, so that a simplified version would read: "Begin, my Muse, and chant what bangs . . ." This kind of inversion recalls the elaborate opening of Milton's *Paradise Lost.* Fergusson uses it here in order to throw emphasis on the last line of the stanza, to give the effect of a ceremonial announcement of the theme, to dress up his poem, and to give it a formal and dignified tone. Throughout the body of the poem Fergusson sustains the note of dignity more quietly and unobtrusively by the occasional use of formal words and phrases; but this note is never again as overdone or inappropriate as it appears in this first stanza.

In the next stanzas the poem moves swiftly forward, and its considerable merits become more evident:

Frae the big stack, weel winnow't on the hill,	
Wi' *divets* theekit frae the weet and drift,	turfs thatched
Sods, peats, and *heath'ry trufs* the chimley fill,	turfs
And gar their thick'ning smeek salute the lift;	smoke; sky
The *gudeman,* new come hame, is blyth to find,	husband
Whan he out o'er the *halland* flings his een,	partition; eyes
That ilka turn is handled to his mind,	every
That a' his housie looks sae cosh and clean;	comfortable
For cleanly house looes he, tho' e'er sae mean.	loves
Weel kens the *gudewife* that the pleughs require	plowmen
A heartsome *meltith,* and refreshing synd	meal; rinse
O' nappy liquor, o'er a bleezing fire:	strong ale
Sair wark and poortith douna weel be join'd.	will not
Wi' butter'd *bannocks* now the *girdle* reeks,	griddle smokes
I' the far nook the *bowie* briskly reams;	small barrel (of
The readied *kail* stand by the chimley cheeks,	cream); rises
And had the riggin het wi' welcome steams,	keep; rafters hot
Whilk than the daintiest kitchen nicer seems.	

In these two stanzas the wealth of intimate and realistic detail combines with the slow, sedate rhythm of the lines to evoke a charming and convincing impression of the cottage, with its blazing hearth, cozy atmosphere, and hearty household smells. Fergusson understands the function of the ninth line in rounding off the meaning of each stanza, and he tends to introduce a more formal touch in these last lines to tighten the stanzaic structure. Unaccustomed as he was to writing in the Spenserian stanza, he is rather self-conscious in his handling of it, and sometimes he overemphasizes the formal pattern of the stanza in this way. There is a slight stiffness and an uneasiness of expression, for example, in such final lines as "For cleanly house looes he, tho' e'er sae mean" and "Whilk than the daintiest kitchen nicer seems." The stanza form itself would have been enough to give the effect of quiet dignity for which Fergusson is striving without the extra note of formality in these ninth lines. In his next two stanzas, however, Fergusson succeeds admirably in his reflections on simple versus luxurious living in bringing in easy, rich Scots idiom, without breaking into a stilted English style when he pauses to point the moral, as Burns invariably does in "The Cotter's Saturday Night."

After a stanza which is one of the most attractive and most smoothly written in the poem, describing in convincing detail the after-supper gossip around the "ingle," Fergusson introduces us to the character of the grandmother. This passage (stanzas 7-9), opening with the delightful line "The fient a chiep's amang the bairnies now," is equally good. Fergusson begins to sketch his finely wrought portrait of the grandmother who tells the children ghost stories, "Whilk touzles a' their tap, and gars them shak wi' fear." His gentle comment in stanza 8 on the superstitious fears of the old woman is genuinely moving in its sensitive understanding of and sympathy with the frailty of old age:

O mock na this, my friends! but rather mourn,
  Ye in life's brawest springs wi' reason clear,
Wi' eild our idle fancies a' return, — old age
  And dim our dolefu' days wi' bairnly fear; — childish
  The mind's ay *cradled* when the *grave* is near.

Fergusson shows in these lines a depth of human understanding and a maturity of insight unusual in so young a poet. He maintains this feeling of sympathy mingled with admiration for the old grandmother's courageous spirit in the next stanza, in which we see the pride she takes in making clothes for the youngsters:

On some feast-day, the *wee-things* buskit braw — dressed finely
  Shall heeze her heart up wi' a silent joy, — lift
Fu' cadgie that her head was up and saw — happy
  Her ain spun cleething on a darling oy, — grandchild
  Careless tho' death shou'd make the feast
    her foy. — farewell feast

With these lines Fergusson closes his little sketch of the grandmother, certainly the most touching and one of the most appealing passages in the poem.

In the next section we get a vivid and intimate glimpse of the "gudeman" as he "streeks him at his ease" on the "deas" (bench), feeding the household pets and giving orders to his lads:

Round him will *badrins* and the *colly* come,	the cat
To wag their tail, and cast a thankfu' eie	
To him wha kindly flings them mony a crum	
O' kebbock whang'd, and dainty fadge to prie;	cheese sliced;
This a' the boon they crave, and a' the fee.	loaf; taste
Frae him the *lads* their morning counsel tak,	
What stacks he wants to thrash, what rigs to till;	ridges, sections of field
How big a birn maun lie on *bassie's* back,	burden; dobbin's
For meal and multure to the *thirling mill.*	mill at which tenant is bound to grind

Then comes the "gudewife's" turn to give her girls their final instructions for the evening:

Niest the gudewife her hireling damsels bids	next
Glowr thro' the byre, and see the hawkies bound,	look; white faced cows
Take tent case *Crummy* tak her wonted tids,	care; cow; fits
And ca' the leglin's treasure on the ground,	knock; milk-pail's
Whilk spills a *kebbuck* nice, or yellow *pound.*	which; cheese

The abundance of carefully chosen familiar details in these stanzas gives them realistic charm and distinction. With the exception of one or two phrases, especially the "hireling damsels" and the "leglin's treasure," which smack of neo-Classical euphemisms, nothing is forced or artificial in these lines; everything is in perfect character. The "gudewife's" reference to the unpredictable personality of the cow, "Crummy," for example, and her warning the girls against Crummy's "wonted tids," is a wonderfully suggestive touch. It is in just such details that the compelling charm of the poem lies. They help to build up the comfortable feeling of reality and intimacy which pervades the description of the entire household.

Following a skillfully executed twelfth stanza, picturing the group around the ingle as a heavy and irresistible drowsiness steals over them and the fire burns itself out, Fergusson ends his poem with a grand stanza of benediction:

Peace to the husbandman and a' his tribe,	
Whase care fells a' our wants frae year to year;	satisfies
Lang may his sock and couter turn the gleyb,	plowshare; coulter
And bauks o' corn bend down wi' laded ear.	unplowed strips of land
May SCOTIA's simmers ay look gay and green,	
Her yellow har'sts frae scowry blasts decreed;	harvests; showery
May a' her tenants sit fu' snug and bien,	prosperous
Frae the hard grip of ails and poortith freed,	poverty
And a lang lasting train o' peaceful hours succeed.	

One this note of simple dignity the poem closes, retaining to the end its sincere, unpretentious mood, and reasserting its quiet note of patriotism.

"The Farmer's Ingle" holds a unique position among Fergusson's poems: it is his only serious, non-satiric work which is really successful. And, for that reason alone, it is of the highest importance as a milestone in Fergusson's career and as a basis for conjecturing what he might have accomplished had he lived longer. From a technical point of view, the poem is by no means his best; it does not rank with "Braid Claith" or "Hallow-fair," for example, in sheer mastery of form and general technique. Nevertheless, Fergusson handles the difficult Spenserian stanza (used here for the first time in a Scottish poem) with sensitivity, if not with ease; and his choice of it for "The Farmer's Ingle" was intelligent, for this verse form is surprisingly well suited to his special purpose in the poem. The stanzaic structure itself provides the formality and restraint which are vital elements in the poem, while the rich vernacular style gives it the homely, realistic touch; and the two work together to create the perfect blend of dignity and simplicity which Fergusson is aiming at.

Much of the poem's power lies in its admirable restraint, a quality conspicuously lacking in "The Cotter's Saturday Night." "The Farmer's Ingle" carries its message and makes its point, not through vapid generalities, nor through preposterous "pastoral" imagery, but through a series of quiet, realistic pictures of eighteenth-century Scottish farm life as it really was. In this sense, the poem represents a further development of the boldly realistic type of Scottish pastoralism which, as we have seen, Fergusson inaugurated in "An Eclogue." "The Farmer's Ingle" is a masterpiece of its kind, and it is sharply distinguished from the scores of nauseating, totally artificial, and unconvincing "effusions" in praise of country life which were pouring from the presses throughout the century. Fergusson gets his effects through the steady accumulation of unspectacular but interesting details, which combine to produce an astonishingly vivid impression of a whole way of life. The entire poem is filled with a sense of the peacefulness, the content, the unchanging routine of the life it portrays, a feeling which is reinforced by the slow, stately rhythm of the stanzas. The characters in the poem are, of course, peasant types, slightly idealized, but, nevertheless, convincing and recognizable; they are portrayed with touching human sympathy and real understanding.

"The Farmer's Ingle" proves beyond any doubt that Fergusson was a sincere and dedicated artist, who looked upon himself as such. It proves further than his range was not limited to comic and satiric verse, that he was capable of writing distinguished poetry on serious themes. Though it is not his very best work in some respects, "The Farmer's Ingle" is certainly one of the most ambitious of his poems, and it suggests, perhaps better than any other single poem, that Fergusson had in him the makings of a truly great poet. It reveals, in short, possibilities of depth and range in Fergusson which, had he lived, might have been fulfilled in many directions. As it stands, "The Farmer's Ingle" is a remarkably mature and brilliant performance, especially when we remember that it was written by a lad of twenty-two. It is perhaps not too much to say that it ranks with the finest poetic treatments of rural life in the language.

VI "The Ghaists"

Fergusson's next Scots poems, "The Ghaists: A Kirk-Yard Eclogue," followed quickly on the heels of "The Farmer's Ingle," appearing in Ruddiman's periodical just a week later, on May 27.

It consists of a debate in sixty-seven heroic couplets between two ghosts, George Heriot (or Herriot) and George Watson, founders of two "hospitals" in Edinburgh for the maintenance and education of poor children, over the "Mortmain Bill," which was a legislative scheme to require the vesting of hospital and other institutional capital in government stock at three per cent, thus greatly reducing the hospitals' revenues. Both of the ghostly "founders" denounce the bill as a betrayal of sacred trust. Based on this ephemeral political issue, "The Ghaists" requires more annotation than any other Fergusson poem to make it intelligible to modern readers; and, despite its undoubted cleverness, the eclogue is lacking in universal appeal. It has little of the deft characterization and abiding human interest of "Plainstanes and Causey," Fergusson's earlier eclogue which it resembles in a superficial way. Like "Plainstanes and Causey," however, the poem influenced Burns in "The Brigs of Ayr," supplying him with the metrical form (pentameter couplets) for his poem, with the idea of a debate between two ghosts, and with the "ancients and moderns" theme, the idea of contrasting the good old days with the corrupt present.

From a purely technical point of view, "The Ghaists" is excellent, being well up to Fergusson's usual high standard of craftsmanship. It begins with a suggestive, eerie description of Greyfriars Churchyard at night:

Whare the braid planes in dowy murmurs wave	gloomy
Their antient taps out o'er the cald, clad grave,	tops
Whare *Geordie Girdwood,* mony a lang-spun day,	
Houkit for gentlest banes the humblest clay,	dug; bones
Twa sheeted ghaists, sae grizly and sae wan,	
'Mang lanely tombs their douff discourse began.	lonely; melancholy

Fergusson identifies the place for his readers by the mention of Geordie Girdwood, grave-digger of Greyfriars and one of the most notable eccentrics in Edinburgh, described by Grosart as "a more than ordinarily drunken-looking, withered, unearthly, little old man, with sore eyes." [12] Fergusson sets the scene briefly but skillfully in these opening lines. The hushed atmosphere of eeriness and the sepulchral tone are well suggested by the frequent long vowel sounds and the slow, deliberate rhythm of the passage. The fourth line, "Houkit for gentlest banes the humblest clay," has an especially strong imaginative force. The sinister effect is intensified in Watson's first speech and rises to a climax of horror in Heriot's description of the disgrace and impending destruction of Scotland, where night birds of evil omen appear in broad daylight:

NATURE has chang'd her course; the birds o' day	
Dosin' in silence on the bending spray,	
While owlets round the craigs at noon-tide flee,	crags
And bludey bawks sit singand on the tree.	bats; singing

In his second speech, Heriot reveals the reason behind his gloomy view of Scotland's present and future:

Black be the day that e'er to England's ground	
Scotland was eikit by the UNION's bond;	added
For mony a menzie of destructive ills	crowd
The country now maun brook frae *mortmain bills* . . .	must

Fergusson is here, no doubt, expressing his own opinion of the Act of Union which, as a patriotic Scot, he resents as a betrayal of national honor and independence. Anti-unionist sentiment was still widespread in Fergusson's day, and lingered on for generations later. It was, of course, perfectly natural for Fergusson, a vernacular poet and part of an intensely nationalistic revival of Scottish poetry, to feel this way. That Fergusson's feelings on the matter were vehement and even bitter is apparent from this speech of Heriot, especially in the last biting line, where he speaks of Scottish boys in his hospital "Starving for England's weel at *three per cent*." Watson, in his third speech, takes a more optimistic point of view, and suggests that if the bill does come to a vote it will surely be defeated on humanitarian grounds. Heriot scoffs at this naïve opinion:

I find, my friend, that ye but little ken,	
There's einow on the earth a set o' men,	even now
Wha, if they get their private pouches lin'd,	pockets
Gie na a winnelstrae for a' mankind;	stalk of grass
They'll sell their country, flae their conscience bare . . .	flay

This disillusioned comment on the motives of politicians is put into the mouth of a dramatic character; yet one feels throughout the eclogue that Heriot, more than Watson, represents Fergusson's own sentiments, and that in this passage he is voicing the author's opinion. In Heriot's final speech, he suggests that on the following night he and Watson arouse the ghost of Sir George Mackenzie, a famous Lord Advocate of by-gone days, and persuade him to take their side and "fleg [frighten] the schemers o' the *mortmain-bill.*" With this threat of ghostly intervention, Fergusson brings the conversation neatly to a close.

As in "An Eclogue," Fergusson handles the heroic couplet with skill and fluency in this poem and manages to sustain an easy, conversational tone despite the rigidity of the verse form. The whole poem is smoothly and competently written; the setting is effective, and the dialogue is artistically arranged. "The Ghaists," in short, is further evidence that Fergusson, except where his style becomes vitiated by the influence of sentimentalism, had by 1773 attained a ripeness of technique, a sure and accomplished craftsmanship remarkable in a poet of twenty-two. On the other hand, "The Ghaists" is lacking in some of Fergusson's most attractive qualities, especially in his rich, concrete delineation of character types. He makes no real attempt to humanize Watson and Heriot as he does Plainstanes and Causey. The two ghosts remain more or less philosophical abstractions without clearly defined personalities, but the tone of their conversation is natural and human enough. This lack of universal human interest weakens "The Ghaists" and prevents it from being a really first-rate political satire like Dryden's "Absalom and Achitophel."

These limitations being granted, however, "The Ghaists" is a striking, trenchant work and a significant milestone in Fergusson's career. In this poem he emerges as a *national* poet in the literal sense; he is reaching out into a new realm, treating a subject of national rather than of purely local or personal significance. He becomes, in this satiric eclogue, a spokesman for the people of Scotland in protesting vigorously against corrupt political schemes and English influence. He looks back regretfully on the old days of sturdy Scottish virtue and heroic independence; and, like Burns, he voices with sharp-edged satire his resentment of the Union as a betrayal of national honor and integrity. This patriotic note becomes increasingly important in Fergusson's poems during 1773. We have noted its presence earlier in such pieces as the "Elegy on Scots Music" and "The Farmer's Ingle," and in scattered passages in other poems. But in "The Ghaists"

Scottish patriotism and independence become a major theme, a theme which Fergusson was to introduce into his poems more and more frequently in the last months of his productive career. This emphasis on Scottish nationalism seems to result from Fergusson's new and larger concept of himself not merely as the poet of *The Weekly Magazine* or of Auld Reekie, but as the poet of Scotland herself and as the voice of her people.

VII "On Seeing a Butterfly in the Street"

Exactly four weeks after the printing of "The Ghaists," Fergusson's next Scots poem, "On Seeing a Butterfly in the Street," appeared in *The Weekly Magazine* on June 24,[13] dated by the author, "*Auld Reikie, June* 21," three days before its publication. This poem resembles the "Ode to the Bee" in its metrical form (tetrameter couplets) and in its type of subject matter, but not in style or general treatment. Like the "Bee," Fergusson's "Butterfly" belongs to the general tradition of eighteenth-century contemplative nature poetry. The idea of comparing the butterfly with the fop seems to have been fairly common in the eighteenth century. Fergusson could have found it, for example, in William Hamilton of Bangour's "The Miss and the Butterfly, A Fable, in the manner of the late Mr. Gay,"[14] a work which he is almost certain to have read. He may also have picked up from the same author the suggestion for his lines on the laird who leaves his country estate and goes to court. Hamilton of Bangour has a similar passage in his English epistle to Ramsay, entitled "Horace, Epistle XVIII, Book I, Imitated."[15] Otherwise, however, Fergusson's poem is fresh and independent, bearing the stamp of his own keen observation.

Fergusson's "Butterfly" is ingeniously organized in three sections (verse paragraphs 1-3, 4-5, 6-7), in each of which the poet regards the butterfly and its human counterparts from a different point of view. The first section is a witty social satire wherein Fergusson compares the butterfly with the fop or "macaroni," the human butterfly. Then the poem takes a cunning twist; before the reader realizes what has happened, the mood of the poem has shifted from mockery to pity of the "Poor Butterfly" who has strayed into the stony, competitive city where he is out of his element. Finally, the poet draws a parallel between the plight of the forlorn butterfly and that of a country laird ruined by courts and political schemers, condemning the utter folly of such misguided people who "dip their spoons in ither's kail." Thus we see that the poem undergoes successive changes in mood and emphasis, from sly mockery, to pity, to serious condemnation. Though ostensibly a poem on the butterfly, it is really a very clever social satire. Except in the last lines, it contains little direct moralizing; its meaning is implied rather than explicit. As in the "Bee," Fergusson meditates on a natural phenomenon and then draws the moral; but in "The Butterfly" his treatment of his material is more imaginative, more original, and far more artistic than in the earlier work.

"On Seeing a Butterfly in the Street" is executed with Fergusson's customary verve and vigor. It begins with a spirited description of the poet's reaction as he first catches sight of the colorful creature:

Daft gowk, in MACARONI dress,	fool
Are ye come here to shew your face,	
Bowden wi' pride o' simmer gloss,	swollen
To cast a dash at REIKIE's cross;	
And glowr at mony twa-legg'd creature,	stare
Flees braw by art, tho' worms by nature?	
Like country LAIRD in city cleeding,	clothing
Ye're come to town to lear' good breeding . . .	learn

These lines and the whole first section of the poem are alive with Fergusson's sparkling wit and his sly, pointed mockery. He takes full advantage of the contrast between the gay, painted butterfly and the homely worm from which it springs, using this contrast to satirize the ostentatious vanity of the fops and dandies who displayed themselves on the streets of Edinburgh. At the end of this section, he gives us an amusing glimpse of butterfly and macaronis alike, fluttering to shelter in the event of a sudden rain-storm:

Like thee they scoug frae street or field,	flee for shelter
An' hap them in a lyther bield;	better shelter
For they war' never made to dree	endure
The adverse gloom o' FORTUNE's eie . . .	eye

The central section of the poem is beautifully and delicately written, with some fine imaginative touches. Fergusson wonders how the poor, misguided butterfly could have exchanged the country, with its "green kail-yeards," its fruits, flowers, and song-birds, for the ugly city, with its sordidness, cruelty, and fierce, competitive spirit:

Can Lintie's music be compar'd	linnet's
Wi' *gruntles* frae the CITY-GUARD?	
Or can our flow'rs at ten hours bell	
The GOWAN or the SPINK excel.	daisy; primrose
Now shou'd our sclates wi' hailstanes ring,	slates
What cabbage fald wad screen your wing?	fold, leaf
Say, fluttering fairy! wer't thy hap	
To light beneath braw Nany's cap,	
Wad she, proud butterfly of May!	
In pity lat you skaithless stay;	unharmed
The fury's glancing frae her ein	eyes
Wad rug your wings o' siller sheen,	tear
That, wae for thee! far, far outvy	woe
Her PARIS ARTIST's finest dye . . .	

This is perhaps the most attractive passage in the entire poem. Fergusson, it will be noted, gets in his usual dig at the City Guard in addition to a sly allusion to the evil smells, the "flow'rs" of Auld Reekie. The picture of the butterfly seeking frantically and in vain among the stony wynds and closes for a "cabbage fald" to creep under during a hail-storm is a superb imaginative stroke, while the sketch of "braw Nany" which follows is equally ingenious and perfectly in keeping with the brilliant satiric tone.

The last section of the poem, though executed with Fergusson's characteristic vigor and precision, tends to weaken the total impression somewhat. The satire is rather too heavy-handed and direct, the mood overly serious to blend harmoniously with the light, witty quality of the first two sections. The final four couplets are especially severe in tone, when Fergusson is describing the tragic disillusionment of the country laird who has come to court to be fleeced by wily politicians:

Till in the end they flae him bare,	
Leave him to poortith, and to care.	poverty
Their fleetching words o'er late he sees,	flattering
He trudges hame, repines and dies.	
Sic be their fa' wha dirk thir ben	fall; slip deep inside

In blackest BUSINESS no their ain;
And may they scad their lips fu' leal, scald; well
That dip their spoons in ither's kail.

Despite this excessively severe conclusion, "On Seeing a Butterfly in the Street" is an admirable poem. It contrasts sharply with Fergusson's "Bee" and with other eighteenth-century pieces of the same contemplative variety, which are usually filled with sententious moralizing, philosophical abstractions and generalizations. For the most part, Fergusson resists the temptation to generalize; he expresses his theme in concrete form not only through his vivid and highly imaginative portrayal of the butterfly itself, but through his drawing of ingenious comparisons between the actions of the butterfly and those of certain human types in certain specific situations. Like "Braid Claith," the poem is largely an attack on pride of dress both in men and women. Fergusson's mockery of feminine vanity, for example, is brilliantly suggested in the picture of the butterfly lighting on "braw Nany's cap" and incurring her envious wrath. Besides this quality of concreteness and this method of attack by implication rather than by insipid moralizing, Fergusson's "Butterfly" shows a vast improvement over the "Bee" in style and, to a lesser extent, in versification. Written in fresh and vigorous Scots idiom, it is undiluted by the obnoxious neo-Classical jargon which clutters up the style of the "Bee"; and Fergusson handles his tetrameter couplets with greater skill and fluency here than he had hitherto shown in this form. His lines read smoothly and effectively throughout, and the whole poem gives the impression of expert and finished artistry.

VIII "Hame Content"

Just two weeks after the "Butterfly," on July 8, another and longer poem in tetrameter couplets, "Hame Content—A Satire," appeared in *The Weekly Magazine*.[10] This work is an explicit attack on materialism, on those Scottish gentlemen and "rich chiels" who waste their days in luxurious idleness, and on those who would sooner dash off to Italy than explore their own estates and enjoy the beauties of their native land. One of Fergusson's most nationalistic poems, it expresses sentiments which were common to virtually all the eighteenth-century revivalists, including Ramsay and Burns. One or two of Fergusson's ideas may have been derived from earlier Scots poetry. The theme of resistance to Italian influence, which we have already noted in "The Daft-Days" and the "Elegy on Scots Music," goes back to Ramsay's "Patie Birnie"; and the idea of comparing the Tiber unfavorably with Scottish rivers was probably suggested by Drummond of Hawthornden's "Forth Feasting." On the other hand, Fergusson's passage beginning "Some daft chiel reads," on Scottish gentry rushing off to Italy, anticipates the third speech of Caesar in Burns's "Twa Dogs"—"At operas and plays."

"Hame Content," rather loosely organized in four divisions, begins with a rigorous attack on unscrupulous money-grubbers, people who waste the best years of their lives in a frenzied pursuit of wealth. Fergusson then describes how he loves to spend long summer days in the country, away from the din and fret of the city, among "cottar fock" and "herds" who live simple, heathlful lives and are unconcerned with the senseless struggle for wealth. He contrasts their wholesome, active way of life with that of the sluggish, pampered rich of the city. He urges the Edinburgh gentry to get out into the open country for some healthful exercise. In the third section of the poem, he imagines some "daft chiel" misunderstanding this advice and dashing off to France and Italy. He then moves into the long patriotic passage on the scenic grandeur and delicate pastoral beauty of Scotland, which he regards as superior to the charms of foreign lands. The final section of the work is devoted to a lament for Hamilton of Bangour whose one great poem, "The Braes of Yarrow," celebrates the beautiful valleys of the Yarrow and Tweed in southeastern Scotland.

From this outline, it may be seen that Fergusson's poem is not very well integrated as to theme. There are too many different ideas in "Hame Content," ideas which Fergusson does not succeed in tying together, except in a very superficial way. If the main theme is indeed "hame content," as it seems to be and as the title suggests, then it is difficult to see why Fergusson begins the poem with a diatribe against money-grubbing. Furthermore, it is hard to see the connection between this frantic, unceasing scramble for wealth and the picture which Fergusson draws in the second section of the sluggishness and pampered sloth of the moneyed classes. The poem, in fact, deals with several different sets of contrasted ideas and relationships which Fergusson fails to combine to create a single and powerful effect. As a result, the poem leaves a vaguely disturbing and confused impression.

The style of "Hame Content" suffers likewise from a lack of integration. Though it is, on the whole, far superior in execution to Fergusson's "Bee," it is seriously weakened in the latter portions by the intrusion of conventional pastoral imagery. The first half of the poem and more is written in Fergusson's vigorous Scots idiom; but in the later sections, where he begins to write about the beauties of Scottish scenery, he slips into a sort of hybrid language, an injudicious combination of the vernacular with the stereotyped formulas of Ramsayesque and English pastoralism. This insipid, hybrid style becomes increasingly apparent in such couplets as the following:

And blaw the reed to kittle strains, — intricate
While echo's tongue commends their pains,

. . . .

Come, FANCY, come, and let us tread
The simmer's flow'ry velvet bed . . .

The utter inappropriateness of such language is, of course, immediately obvious. Though it creeps in only toward the close of the poem, it is especially unfortunate since it leaves the reader with an impression of insipid and artificial style. Here again, Fergusson ends his poem with a conventional passage in an effort to bring his work into touch with the mainstream of eighteenth-century poetic tradition.

The earlier parts of "Hame Content," on the other hand, are executed with Fergusson's characteristic dash and strong originality. Such lines as the following bear the unmistakable mark of his artistic personality:

Some daft chiel reads, and takes advice; — fellow
The chaise is yokit in a trice; — harnessed
Awa drives he like huntit de'il, — devil
And scarce tholes TIME to cool his wheel, — allows
Till he's Lord kens how far away,
At Italy, or Well o' Spaw,

. . . .

There rest him weel; for eith can we — easily
Spare mony glakit gouks like he; — silly fools

. . . .

The ARNO and the TIBUR lang
Hae run fell clear in Roman sang;
But, save the reverence of schools!
They're baith but lifeless dowy pools. — gloomy

This is spirited poetry, and it shows Fergusson handling the tetrameter couplet with an ease and mastery which he had not hitherto attained in this meter. His lines have a biting, sarcastic force reminiscent of "Braid Claith."

"Hame Content" resembles "Braid Claith" in its explicit, direct satirical method, but it falls below "Braid Claith" as a work of art because it lacks a single-minded purpose, a unified theme, and a well-integrated style. Many parts of it are brilliantly written; but, on the whole, it is a rather disappointing poem.

IX "Leith Races"

Fergusson's next poem, however, "Leith Races," is an undoubted masterpiece. It appeared in *The Weekly Magazine* two weeks after "Hame Content," on July 22, dated by Fergusson, "*Auld Reikie, July* 21." Thus the poem was apparently finished just one day before it was published by Ruddiman. "Leith Races" is Fergusson's second longest vernacular poem, and it is one of his best. In a sense, it is a companion piece to "Hallow-fair," being in the "Christis Kirk" stanza and descriptive of another Edinburgh festival. The Leith Races were the social highlight of the summer season in Old Edinburgh. They were an annual series of horse races, with elaborate civic ceremonies, held during an entire week in July on the Leith Sands, about three miles from the city. The citizens of Auld Reekie flocked *en masse* down to Leith in holiday mood to witness the festivities, and many shops and businesses in the city closed for the whole week of the "Races." Fergusson gives a wonderfully vivid and exuberant picture, touched with inimitable satire, of the whole crowded and boisterous scene.

"Leith Races," like "Hallow-fair," is in the pure tradition of "Christis Kirk" in its kind of subject matter and in its general method, though again, as in "Hallow-fair," Fergusson uses his modified form of the traditional stanza with four instead of two rimes in the octave. As for its details, the poem gives us Fergusson's firsthand, imaginative observations of the "Races" and is wholly independent of earlier poetry. On the other hand, "Leith Races" had a powerful influence on several later Scots poems, most notably on Burns's great satiric masterpiece, "The Holy Fair." In this work, Burns uses Fergusson's stanza and follows the method of "Leith Races" step by step, introducing his poem with a vision of "Fun," which corresponds with Fergusson's "Mirth" and performs exactly the same function in the poem. "The Holy Fair" is more exclusively satiric in intention, more mature and penetrative in its imaginative power and grasp of the whole scene than "Leith Races"; and it surpasses Fergusson's poem in its sheer technical brilliance and incomparable expressiveness. However, had it not been for the example of fine artistry and compelling charm which Fergusson set in "Leith Races," Burns's "Holy Fair" might never have been written, or at least would have taken different form, and would not, perhaps, have been the great poem that it is.

In structure, "Leith Races" falls into four main divisions. The first five stanzas form the introduction and present Fergusson's meeting and conversation with "Mirth," the mythological figure who offers to take him to the "Races" and to show him the amusing sights to be found there. In stanzas 6 to 13, Fergusson describes various types of people preparing to go to the races or on their way there: the fashionable ladies dressing up for the occasion; the barking peddlers hawking "true an' faithfu' lists" of the horses running that day; the City Guardsmen being shaved and inspected for the races; the drunken "tinkler billies" reeling down Leith Walk; and the inevitable "browster wives" busily getting out their cheapest and sourest ale and whisky which, in spite of its poor quality, is sure to sell during this thirsty season. In stanzas 14 to 19, we are given vivid glimpses of the tumultuous scene on Leith Sands, where "Buchan bodies" cry their fish through the crowds; dishonest gamblers huddle over games of dice and "Rowly Powl"; horses and carriages dash to and fro in every direction; the Lord Lyon King of Arms asserts his authority; the town guard lines up the horses for the races; and young fellows from the Robinhood debating club engage in "lang and dreech [wearisome] contesting." In stanza 20, Fergusson closes the poem, describing the drunken aftermath of the races and ending on a whimsical note of warning against the City Guard.

The structural method here is obviously Fergusson's usual one of lighting up carefully chosen dramatic details picked out from the general confusion with unerring skill to give a lively and concrete impression of the whole. More specifically, it is the method he had used with great success in "Hallow-fair," though here it will be noted that he lays more emphasis on preparations for the festivities and less on their aftermath. "Leith Races" is the longer poem, giving a fuller and more detailed picture; and, as a result, Fergusson's structural method works, if anything, even more successfully in this poem than in "Hallow-fair," his earlier masterpiece in this style.

It is no wonder that Burns was fascinated by the vision of "Mirth" in the first five stanzas of "Leith Races," for it is one of the most delightful passages in all Fergusson. He manipulates the rollicking meter in this introduction and throughout the poem with the same ease and versatile skill which we have already noticed in "Hallow-fair." The introduction of "Mirth" is a master stroke of imagination. Fergusson gives to this abstraction a most engaging and natural character perfectly adapted to the humorous context of the poem as a whole. His "Mirth" contrasts significantly with the pompous abstract figures usually found in philosophical "vision" poetry, a poetic tradition which Fergusson may be incidentally satirizing. At any rate, "Mirth" is a thoroughly charming, vivacious creature; and the poet is only too ready to accept her offer to accompany him to the races. The fifth stanza, where Fergusson agrees to "Mirth's" proposition, is especially vigorous, full of zest and sparkle, and executed with superb craftsmanship:

A bargain be't, and, by my feggs,	faith
Gif ye will be my mate,	if
Wi' you I'll screw the cheery pegs,	tune the fiddle
Ye shanna find me blate;	shy
We'll reel an' ramble thro' the sands,	
And jeer wi' a' we meet;	
Nor hip the daft and gleesome bands	miss
That fill EDINA's street	Edinburgh's
Sae thrang this day.	crowded

Here is Fergusson in his most brilliant and characteristic vein. His lines have a wonderfully swift, exhilarating rhythm to them; they sing their way into the memory, aided by artfully placed alliteration in lines 1 and 5 and by the recurrence of the "ee" sound throughout. Fergusson's facile mastery of the vernacular idiom and his sensitive grasp of poetic technique are, in fact, nowhere more evident than in this poem.

In stanza 6, Fergusson plunges us into the actual activities of the day. In the long series of stanzas which follows, the significant technical details, the fine imaginative touches, and the bold descriptive devices are too numerous for individual analysis. A few general observations on Fergusson's performance in the body of the poem may be made, however, and one or two typical passages singled out for comment. In general, Fergusson follows rather closely the descriptive method he had used in "Hallow-fair"; he shifts rapidly from scene to scene, portraying the boisterous actions, noises, and characters of the day through focussing attention on judiciously chosen concrete details. As in "Hallow-fair," for example, he gives us direct quotations to render the vocal background more vivid, uses northern dialect in stanzas dealing with Highland types, and introduces some of the same character types: the coy girl, the Aberdeenshire peddler, the tricksters and frauds, the "browster wives," and the inevitable City Guard.

The stanzas on the City Guard are indeed some of the most effective in "Leith Races":

To Whisky Plooks that brunt for wooks — pimples; burned; weeks
On town-guard soldiers faces,
Their barber bauld his whittle crooks, — knife
An' scrapes them for the races:
Their Stumps erst us'd to *filipegs*, — legs; kilts
Are dight in spaterdashes — dressed
Whase barkent hides scarce fend their legs — encrusted
Frae weet, and weary plashes — splashes
O' dirt that day.
(stanza 8)

We next see the captain inspecting the Guard and advising his men to be particularly careful in handling the hostile crowds; Fergusson then makes his own wry comment on the Highlanders' unpopularity:

Her *Nanesel* maun be carefu' now,	own self
Nor maun she pe misleard,	be unmannerly
Sin baxter lads hae seal'd a vow	baker
To skelp and clout the guard:	beat
I'm sure AULD REIKIE kens o' nane	
That wou'd be sorry at it,	
Tho' they should dearly pay the kane,	penalty
An' get their tails weel sautit	salted
And sair thir days.	these
(stanza 10)	

These stanzas show Fergusson at his liveliest, lashing out at his old enemy, the Guard, in bold and irresistibly comic style. His use of internal rime in the first line of stanza 8, "To WHISKY PLOOKS that brunt for wooks," deftly sets the tone of impish mockery, a tone that is sustained through his alliterative phrases ("barber bauld," "weet, and weary," "dirt that day"). The refererence to "their barber bauld" is a fine artistic touch, a perfect choice of epithet, striking as it does the exact note of mock-heroic satire at which Fergusson is aiming. In the next stanza, Fergusson gives us the captain's speech to the Guard directly quoted in heavy Highland accent, while in the first lines of stanza 10, given above, he mimics the guardsmen's uncouth Highland speech in his spelling of the word "be" as "pe" and in the characteristic expression "Her *Nanesel.*" On the whole, these stanzas on the Guard are powerfully and imaginatively conceived, and are written with a subtle artistry which even Burns, in his best satiric poems, scarcely surpasses. Though Fergusson does not sustain this high level of excellence in all twenty stanzas of his poem, he never drops far below it. His exhilarating comic style and ripe craftsmanship never falter for a moment; "Leith Races" is, in fact, the most consistently brilliant of his longer poems.

X *A Look Backwood*

With "Leith Races" Fergusson reached the top level of his achievement as a writer of poetry which was both sharply realistic in method and comic in mood. In the five short months of productive life left to him, he was perhaps to equal but never to surpass his performance in this superb extravaganza of Edinburgh life; but, given a few more years of experience, there is every reason to believe that he would have attained even greater accomplishments. Looking back over the work he produced during the first seven months of 1773, we see that, far from showing any signs of exhaustion, Fergusson was rapidly expanding his range, experimenting with new forms and subject matters, and writing with increasing vitality and steadily improving technique. There is a decided tendency toward greater variety in verse forms during these months. In "Plainstanes and Causey," for example, Fergusson reverted to the tetrameter couplet, and handled it with gradually increasing mastery in the "Bee," the "Butterfly," and "Hame Content." During the same period he used his favorite "Habbie" stanza in only three poems, "Caller Water," "The Rising of the Session," and "To Andrew Gray." In "The Ghaists" he gained further experience in the heroic couplet, while in "The Farmer's Ingle" he made an entirely new and daring experiment with Spenserian stanzas, an experiment which is eminently successful. Finally, in "Leith Races" he managed the difficult "Christis Kirk" stanza with even greater skill than he had shown in "Hallow-fair." This eagerness to diversify his work, to try out new verse forms and master them, is indicative of Fergusson's creative vitality.

With regard to subject matter and treatment, he showed the same experimental spirit. He had achieved his first real success in poems of humorous social description; and he continued to develop this genre in "Caller Water," "Plainstanes and Causey," "The Rising of the Session," the "Butterfly," and "Leith Races." At the same time, he began to branch out into new genres, attempting the contemplative nature poem in the "Bee" and "Butterfly"; the poem of serious social description in "The Farmer's Ingle"; the political satire in "The Ghaists"; and a more serious type of social satire in "Hame Content," a development of the earlier "Braid Claith." These poems must be regarded as attempts by Fergusson to widen his scope and to dignify his position as a national poet. It is interesting to note that, whereas in his comic poetry Fergusson had by the middle of 1773 gone far beyond the poetic conventions of his day and had established a daringly original and distinctive literary personality of his own, in his more serious poems, where he was just beginning to feel his way into unfamiliar genres, he was much more conventional, more closely bound to the accepted poetic norms of the eighteenth century.

On the whole, Fergusson's work during these months gives one the impression that he was a young poet of twenty-two who had a great and expanding future. He was producing distinguished poetry at a prolific rate, experimenting with new forms and genres, and showing increasing vitality and maturity. Fergusson's new maturity in this period reveals itself in his increasing tendency to interpret his observations and to criticize the life and social manners around him rather than merely to record them. The beginnings of this urge to interpret and criticize were observed in some of his earlier poems, especially in "Braid Claith"; but, during the first half of 1773, this intellectual awareness in Fergusson, this tendency to evaluate his experience, was definitely on the increase and made itself felt not just occasionally but in poem after poem—in "Plainstanes and Causey," "The Rising of the Session," "The Farmer's Ingle," "The Ghaists," the "Butterfly," and "Hame Content" in particular. During this same period, along with this interpretive and critical tendency in Fergusson, there is a corresponding tendency to broaden the scope and significance of his subject matters. In such poems as "The Farmer's Ingle," "The Ghaists," and "Hame Content," for example, Fergusson introduced strongly nationalistic themes. He was beginning to write on subjects of national rather than purely local significance. Finally, he continued to make distinguished and meaningful poetry out of the most ordinary materials of everyday life, a rare achievement in any age, but especially rare in the eighteenth century. In his astonishingly effective use of intimate, homely, realistic detail, he anticipated the work of Burns. His achievement during these few months is impressive in itself, but even more significant for the promise that it holds of greater things to come.

CHAPTER 5

Scots Poems of 1773:
"Ode to the Gowdspink" to "Auld Reikie"

AULD REIKIE, wale o' ilka Town
That SCOTLAND kens beneath the Moon . . .
FERGUSSON

I "Ode to the Gowdspink"

AFTER "Leith Races," Fergusson tried his hand for the third time at the didactic nature poem with his "Ode to the Gowdspink." It appeared in Ruddiman's *Weekly Magazine* on August 12, over the usual signature, and was dated by the author, "*North-Belton, Aug.* 9," indicating that this poem, like the "Bee," was written during one of Fergusson's week-end excursions. Here again, as in the "Bee" and the "Butterfly," he uses the tetrameter couplet. The poem describes the "gowdspink" (goldfinch) under contrasting free and caged conditions, and it ends with some general observations on the value of personal liberty. The idea of using the wild song-bird as a symbol for the joys of liberty is, of course, a common enough poetic device.

The "Ode to the Gowdspink" is fairly neatly constructed. It begins with a glowing description of the bird in its wild, natural surroundings. Then Fergusson pauses to make a moral point which he had touched on earlier in "Hame Content":

'Mang man, wae's-heart! we aften find — alas
The brawest drest want peace of mind, — finest
While he that gangs wi' ragged coat — goes
Is weil contentit wi' his lot.

This moral applies to the goldfinch too: his beauty is often his misfortune since, as the loveliest of Scottish song-birds, he is the most often trapped and caged. The caged bird, miserable in the midst of comfort, envies his free brothers. At this point, Fergusson pauses again to apostrophize "Liberty." He then returns to the goldfinch again and develops further the Miltonic contrast (see *Samson Agonistes,* lines 268-71) between luxurious confinement and strenuous freedom. In his final verse-paragraph, he sums up briefly the philosophic theme of the poem: life without liberty is not worth living. The structural principle which Fergusson uses is, of course, a rather obvious and conventional one. He describes the beauty and misfortunes of the bird, pausing every now and then to point the obvious moral. As in the "Bee," he tends to overwork this heavily didactic element.

On the other hand, the "Gowdspink" is a much better executed poem than the "Bee," though it is not so good as the "Butterfly." Fergusson's descriptions of the bird are generally quite effective, while even the conventional philosophic passages have a degree of freshness because they are expressed in Scots. Fergusson's tendency, so noticeable in the "Bee," to lapse into standard English whenever he starts to moralize is less apparent here, though it shows up in an occasional hackneyed choice of word, and in one or two decidedly flat couplets, such as

Ah, Liberty! thou bonny dame,
How wildly wanton is thy stream . . .

On the whole, however, the poem is characterized by a more genuinely lyrical quality than these lines would indicate and by a spirited feeling for nature which is unquestionably sincere. This quality of sincerity, together with Fergusson's usual keen observation and vigorous style, distinguishes the poem from the hundreds of such didactic nature poems of the era and saves it from being merely a conventional exercise. The uninhibited outdoor atmosphere of the open countryside that always delighted Fergusson is pleasingly evoked in this poem, especially in the following breezy lines:

The Gowdspink chatters joyous here,
And courts wi' gleesome sangs his peer:
The MAVIS frae the new-bloom'd thorn — song-thrush
Begins his *lauds* at earest morn; — earliest
And herd lowns louping o'er the grass, — fellows frisking
Needs far less fleetching till his lass, — flattering, coaxing to

Than paughty damsels bred at courts,	haughty
Wha thraw their mou's, and take the dorts . . .	twist; are disdainful, sullen

The "Gowdspink" is a prime example of Fergusson's developing originality as a writer on serious themes, of his gradual working away from and beyond the genteel convention and yet remaining within it. In the earlier "Bee," Fergusson was making his first cautious experiment in a well-established genre and was writing, for the most part, in the ready-made, artificial style associated with it; but in the "Gowdspink," he shows more confidence, more freshness, and more vigor in his expression. He is, in short, while remaining clearly in the accepted genre, beginning to develop his own individual style, to express his own artistic personality within the framework of the convention. Thus, though by no means one of his best works, the "Gowdspink" proves that Fergusson was moving in the right direction and suggests, together with the "Butterfly" and, especially, "The Farmer's Ingle," that he had within him the imaginative instinct of a first-rate literary artist.

In looking back over Fergusson's three poems in this genre, his "Bee," "Butterfly," and "Gowdspink," we are struck by the fact that whatever freshness or merit these pieces contain seems to result from their *personal* quality, their relevance to Fergusson's own experience. In all three, there are strong suggestions that Fergusson chose to write on these subjects not from a blind desire to follow poetic conventions of his day, but because he was driven to do so through an emotional reaction to his own difficult and discouraging situation in life. These poems have at times a subjective tone which is definitely Romantic and anticipates the powerful subjectivity of such Romantic lyrics as Shelley's "To a Skylark" or Wordsworth's "I Wandered Lonely as a Cloud." It is significant that all three Fergusson poems take on freshness and vigor whenever this underlying personal element is introduced. The "Bee," for example, rises above the commonplace only at the end where Fergusson expresses what amounts to a personal confession of faith in himself as a poet and in the immortality of poetic achievement. Similarly, in the "Butterfly," though Fergusson perhaps never identifies himself consciously with the insect, the plight of the beautiful, fragile creature wandering out of his natural element among the stony, unsympathetic streets of the city, is obviously comparable to Fergusson's own unlucky destiny.

In the "Gowdspink," finally, the personal element is perhaps even more clearly at work. Fergusson's sympathetic and genuinely moving picture of the caged bird reminds one again of the impoverished poet himself: his mind filled with an incalculable potential of compelling poetic ideas and with a driving urge to pour them out in tangible artistic form; yet hampered, confined, and driven to distraction by the sheer necessity of earning his daily bread; forced to dissipate the greater part of his time and energy in the gloomy, stuffy cage of the Commissary Office, while his spirit hungered for the open fields and an opportunity to cultivate its powers in dignity and freedom. Again it is the genuineness of feeling, the underlying personal emotion, which gives this poem its freshness and distinction, which sets it apart from the conventional run of eighteenth-century exercises in this genre.

II "To the Principal and Professors"

Three weeks after the "Gowdspink," Fergusson produced another comic masterpiece entitled, "To the Principal and Professors of the University of St Andrews, on their superb treat to Dr Samuel Johnson." This poem, in tetrameter couplets, was dated by Fergusson, "*Edin. Sept.* 1," and appeared in *The Weekly Magazine* on the next day, September 2. The occasion of the poem was the visit of Johnson and Boswell to St. Andrews on August 19, 1773, where they were royally entertained by the faculty with an elaborate feast in their honor. Fergusson, who seems to have disliked Johnson, resents this ostentatious show of hospitality to a man who had insulted Scotland and Scotsmen on numerous occasions. He wishes that he could have been there and in charge of the arrangements; then there would have been no expensive foreign dishes for the visiting celebrities, only good, plain Scottish fare. And he gives his own whimsical suggestions for a suitable menu for "Samy," with the haggis—a national dish almost inevitably revolting to foreigners—appropriately at the top of the list. This passage probably gave Burns the original inspiration for his famous "Address to a Haggis."

Fergusson's poem starts off with tremendous vigor and keen, sarcastic wit:

St Andrews town may look right gawsy,	stately
Nae Grass will grow upon her cawsey,	street
Nor wa'-flow'rs of a yellow dye,	wall
Glour dowy o'er her Ruins high,	look sadly
Sin Samy's head weel pang'd wi' lear,	since; crammed;
Has seen the Alma mater there:	learning
Regents, my winsome billy boys!	fellows
'Bout him you've made an unco noise . . .	remarkable

The comic effect of these animated opening lines comes largely from the ludicrous familiarity with which Fergusson refers to "Samy," the revered Dr. Johnson, and addresses the learned "Regents," or professors, of St. Andrews—an irreverent audacity that reminds us of Fergusson's undergraduate days and of his "Elegy on Gregory." He goes on to mock the toadying attitude of the regents toward Johnson: they made such a fuss over him in the hope of keeping him for a long visit "on the Fifan border," that is at St. Andrews, in order to enhance their own prestige. He next imagines what the dinner must have been like, with fancy French dishes, including "crieshy soup," "*snails,*" and "*puddocks*" (frogs). Then he introduces his own suggested menu in a brilliant passage full of irrepressible Fergussonian waggery:

But hear me lads! gin I'd been there,	if
How I wad trimm'd the bill o' fare!	
For ne'er sic surly wight as he	such
Had met wi' sic respect frae me.	
Mind ye what Sam, the lying loun!	rascal
Has in his Dictionar laid down?	
That Aits in England are a feast	oats
To cow an' horse, an' sican beast,	such a
While in Scots ground this growth was common	
To gust the gab o' Man an' Woman.	please the palate
Tak tent, ye Regents! then, an' hear	heed
My list o' gudely hamel gear,	home-bred stuff
Sic as ha'e often rax'd the wyme	stretched;
O' blyther fallows mony time;	stomach
Mair hardy, souple, steive an' swank,	sturdy; limber
Than ever stood on Samy's shank.	

Here, Fergusson, it will be noted, paraphrases quite literally

Johnson's notorious definition of "oats" and turns it to good, humorous account. The whole passage is executed with extraordinary dash and gusto, with a rich, humorous force which seems to anticipate the style of Burns's "Tam O' Shanter." Fergusson's alliterative line, "Mair hardy, souple, steive, an' swank," for example, is unsurpassed for sheer vigor of expression.[1] His couplets in this passage flow along briskly and forcefully, with natural rhythm and emphasis, and yet are perfectly regular in form. This ability to create a spirited conversational tone within the rigid discipline of a poetic form—which we have noted before as one of Fergusson's rarest gifts—is nowhere more apparent than in this poem. Fergusson immediately gives his proposed menu in another splendidly vigorous passage:

Imprimis, then, a haggis fat
Weel tottl'd in a seything pat, — boiled; boiling pot
Wi' *spice* and *ingans* well ca'd thro' — onions; spread
Had help'd to gust the stirrah's mow, — fellow's mouth
And plac'd itsel in truncher clean — wooden platter
Before the gilpy's glowrin een. — rascal's; eyes

. . . .

Then let his wisdom girn an' snarl — grimace
O'er a weel-tostit girdle farl . . . — griddled oat-cake

Fergusson outlines his whimsical "bill o' fare" with an enthusiasm which is wholly delightful, while the picture he draws of the great, pompous Dr. Johnson "girning" and snarling over a "farl" and wheezing over the "contents o' sma' ale quegh" (small ale cup) is irresistibly funny.

After a complimentary reference to Drummond of Hawthornden, Fergusson sums up the serious point of his address in a neatly turned verse paragraph; and then, with unaccountably poor judgment, he tacks on two more verse paragraphs at the end which are entirely irrelevant to his theme. These form a witty public answer to an eccentric gentleman in Dunfermline who, incensed at Fergusson's uncomplimentary remarks on Fife in his English poem "An Expedition to Fife" (*Weekly Magazine*, August 26, 1773), had formally challenged the poet to a duel. Although this by-play is amusing enough in itself, it obviously has no bearing on Fergusson's ridicule of Johnson and the professors, and it mars the artistic integrity of an otherwise first-rate little satire.

If we disregard this final section, "To the Principal and Professors" ranks fairly high among Fergusson's comic pieces. The imaginative appeal of the whole concept, the ingenuity of Fergusson's satiric method, and, above all, his powerful and effective style all work together to raise the poem above the commonplace, to make it something more than a clever satire on a long-forgotten occasion. In breadth of appeal it is a decided improvement over "The Ghaists," that other satire Fergusson wrote on an ephemeral issue, even when we admit that "To the Principal and Professors" depends for part of its interest on our present-day knowledge of Johnson's character. It illustrates as well as any other poem Fergusson's daring originality, his characteristic playfulness, and his independent, irreverent attitude toward established authority. It also shows that, as Fergusson gained experience and confidence in his own powers as a poet, his satire became increasingly bold and outspoken and more and more specific in its application.

III "The Election"

Two weeks later on September 16, appeared "The Election," Fergusson's third and last poem in the "Christis Kirk" stanza and altogether one of his finest performances. It was published in *The Weekly Magazine* apparently three days after its completion, since it is signed: "R. Fergusson. *Auld Reikie,* Sept. 13." The poem is a socio-political satire, describing from a humorous point of view a municipal election in Edinburgh—or rather that part of the election which involved the choosing of "deacons," the representatives of the fourteen incorporated "trades" of Edinburgh in the Town Council.[2] It is the first political satire to be written in the "Christis Kirk" form and represents, therefore, a significant extension in the subject matter of the genre. Here again Fergusson was breaking the ground for Burns, who followed Fergusson's lead and made a similar extension of the tradition in his "Ordination," a satire on church politics in the "Christis Kirk" stanza. Burns was further indebted to "The Election" for the name of his "Souter Johnie" in "Tam O'

Shanter" (from Fergusson's "souter Jock"), for two lines (147-48) in "The Twa Dogs" which echo Fergusson's fourteenth stanza, and for a passage in "A Mauchline Wedding." [3]

In "The Election" Fergusson introduced his second modification of the "Christis Kirk" stanza. The traditional rime scheme was A B A B / A B A B / C, and we have noted how Fergusson added two rimes to the octave in "Hallow-fair" and "Leith Races": A B A B / C D C D / E. In this poem he attempts a compromise between the two forms, using three instead of four rimes in the octave and thereby linking the rime schemes of the two quatrains as follows: A B A B / A C A C / D. This interesting and hitherto unnoticed variation in "The Election" is further evidence of the poet's continuing willingness to experiment, to try out new forms of his own in the search for a perfect balance, an ideal medium.

In this poem Fergusson employs the same structural method which he had used so effectively in "Hallow-fair," "Leith Races," and other poems. He presents a lively series of individual vignettes (ingeniously linked) to build up a concrete impression of the scene as a whole. And in "The Election," the first of these vignettes, in which we see and hear the pompous, domineering little citizen getting himself spruced up for the deacons' dinner, is one of the most inimitable and delightful passages in all Fergusson:

Haste, EPPS, quo' John, an' bring my gez,	wig
Tak tent ye dinna't spulzie:	care; spoil
Last night the barber ga't a friz,	curl
An' straikit it wi' ulzie.	stroked; oil
Hae done your PARITCH lassie *Liz,*	porridge
Gi'e me my sark an' gravat;	shirt; tie
I'se be as braw's the Deacon is	I'll
When he taks AFFIDAVIT	
O' FAITH the day.	

Whar's *Johnny* gaun, cries neebor BESS,	going
That he's sae gayly bodin	arrayed
Wi' new kam'd wig, weel syndet face,	combed; washed
Silk hose, for hamely hodin?	homespun cloth
"Our Johny's nae sma' drink you'll guess,	
"He's trig as ony muir-cock,	spruce; moor
"An' forth to mak a Deacon, lass;	

"He downa speak to poor fock	will not
Like us the day."	

In a few masterful strokes, and entirely through dialogue, Fergusson suggests in these stanzas the whole character of the man, his ludicrous vanity and self-importance. The reader gets a wonderfully vivid impression of the little fellow bustling about, ordering the servants around, proudly commenting on his newly-groomed wig, and predicting that he will be "as braw's the Deacon" on this great occasion. This second stanza is, in fact, a brilliant little dramatic monologue. The taunting remarks of the neighbors in stanza 3, as Johnny steps forth starched and spruce in his unaccustomed finery, sound authentic and convincing and are perfectly calculated to drive home the satiric point of the sketch. The whole passage is concrete and dramatic in effect.

Fergusson's astonishing ability to create lively characters in a few short lines is nowhere more apparent than here. His economy of expression and the superb naturalness of his dialogue are equally remarkable, especially when we consider that he is working within a difficult and complex verse form. In spite of the exigencies of the "Christis Kirk" stanza, however, the dialogue rings true and is handled with extraordinary vigor, aided by the familiar allusions to household matters, as in the line, "Hae done your PARITCH lassie *Liz,*" and by Fergusson's use of richly colloquial idiom, as in the expression, "nae sma' drink," meaning "no unimportant person."

In the fifth stanza, we are presented with another shrewdly drawn picture, this time of the cobbler's transformation:

The canty cobler quats his sta',	happy; quits; stall
His ROZET an' his LINGANS;	wax and thread
His buik has dree'd a sair, sair fa'	body; suffered; fall
Frae meals o' BREAD an' INGANS:	onions
Now he's a pow o' WIT and LAW,	head
An' taunts at soals an' heels;	soles
To WALKER's he can rin awa,	
There whang his CREAMS an' JEELS	slice; jellies
Wi' life that day.	zest

Here is Fergusson's comic imagination at its finest. His satire, in this sensitive portrait of the cobbler, takes on a kindlier, almost pathetic tone, without losing anything of its trenchant, objective force. He pictures the poor fellow's enthusiasm as he looks forward to a hearty meal and to lavish entertainment at the deacons' banquet, a refreshing change after months of drudgery and malnutrition. On this day alone he suddenly and temporarily becomes a person of importance, "a pow o' WIT and LAW," and can afford for a few triumphant hours to "taunt at soals an' heels," the humble symbols of his trade.

The splendid verve of the opening section is well sustained through the next two groups of stanzas on the feast and its aftermath. The whole scene of enthusiastic gluttony, rowdiness, freakish wit, and bestiality is laid before us with relentless realism. There is, indeed, a degree of coarseness in some of Fergusson's details, especially in stanza 6 and the last three lines of stanza 10. But the emphasis on the sheer vulgarity of election celebrations is an essential part of Fergusson's satiric method, and the element of coarseness is, on that account, justified. In the description of the feast, Fergusson's humor is based largely on his imaginative observation and his portrayal of certain incongruities. His satiric intention comes out clearly in such sly comments as "The grace is said—its no o'er lang," and less obviously, but more powerfully in the deacon's toast: "Come, here's our NOBLE SEL's / WEEL MET the day." The point of the satire lies in the contrast between the deacon's saying grace and uttering these "noble" sentiments and the very ignoble and abandoned behavior of himself and the whole company.

Similarly, in the magnificent, metaphorical speech of "cooper Will," the humor comes from the utter incongruity of Will's rhetorical manner of speaking and of the frank vulgarity of what he is actually saying. Here, as in the sketch of the cobbler, Fergusson uses the symbols of the man's trade to good, comic effect. The cooper speaks quite appropriately in terms of barrels and "girds" (hoops), voicing his determination to give his barrel (stomach) a rousing good "sweel," while, at the same time, guaranteeing that he will not cast "ae gird."

The episode of "souter Jock" is given the same broadly humorous treatment. Reeling home from the party, Jock falls by accident into the wrong bed, the one in which Will's wife is lying. Will, who finds them there, takes dire vengeance, first on Jock, and then on his wife, Maggie:

Syne wi' a muckle alshin lang — then; cobbler's awl
He brodit MAGGIE's hurdies; — pricked; buttocks
An' 'cause he thought her i' the wrang,
There pass'd nae bonny wordies
'Mang them that night.

After the description of this barbarous punishment, Fergusson's arch comment on "nae bonny wordies" comes as a magnificent bit of comic understatement. The following stanza, with Fergusson's shrewd reflections on the good-natured reconciliation between Will and his wife and Jock when they sober up next morning, is equally amusing.

The gusto and dazzling fluency of Fergusson's style carry the reader through the last three stanzas of "The Election." There is no falling off in quality, no lapsing into conventional generalities toward the end as in many of his poems. In stanza 13, there occurs one of Fergusson's fine imaginative touches, when he pictures dishonest voters taking half-crown bribes from politicians. He observes that the recipients of this tainted money never stop to check the coins for correct weight:

They pouch the gowd, nor fash the town — pocket; gold; bother
For weights an' scales to weigh them
Exact that day.

In this ingenious way, Fergusson suggests to the imagination of his reader the darkness and furtiveness of these nefarious transactions: the voter quickly pockets his half-crown and slinks guiltily off. This kind of suggestiveness, highly characteristic of Fergusson's style in general, helps to give richness of texture to his verse. The final stanza of "The Election" is remarkable for one especially brilliant figure of speech, as Fergusson comments on the dire effects of this hard drinking season on the deacons:

For tho' ev'now they look right bluff,
Sic drinks, 'ere HILLOCKS meet, — before
Will hap some Deacons in a truff, — cover; turf
Inrow'd in the lang leet — enrolled; list
O' death yon night.

The phrase "lang leet" (from the French "élite") is superbly appropriate here, since it was a technical term for the preliminary, unshortened list of six candidates for an Edinburgh deaconship. In this highly suggestive image, Fergusson expresses the deacons' mortality in terms of the election, imagining the deacons' names being enrolled in the "lang leet," the endless list of death.

On the whole, "The Election" is a very impressive poem. For sheer exuberance and creative vitality it is unsurpassed among Fergusson's poems. Fergusson's technique is consistently good, while his handling of the dialogue in stanzas 2 and 3 shows a facile mastery of his artistic medium which goes beyond anything of the kind that he had done so far. "The Election," moreover, is more purely satirical in purpose than either "Hallow-fair" or "Leith Races"; and it gives evidence of Fergusson's characteristic fearlessness, his clear-sighted, objective vision in criticizing political as well as social abuses. It is, of course, primarily entertaining rather than didactic; but it does show that Fergusson was very much aware of the shortcomings in the politics and society of his day and made conscious efforts to expose them in the light of his satiric imagination. Here again his "Election" points forward to the satires of Burns.

The poem is, finally, remarkable for its realism, for its relentless presentation of the sordid, as well as the genial side of the election festivities. In this respect the poem anticipates the method of Fergusson's last masterpiece, "Auld Reikie." Indeed, Henley and Henderson's famous description of Burns's "Jolly Beggars" as an "irrestible presentation of humanity caught in the act and summarized for ever in the terms of art" [4] could be applied without undue exaggeration to this poem of Fergusson. By and large, "The Election" is a splendid performance, intensely human in its appeal, and undoubtedly one of Fergusson's most fascinating and powerful poems.

IV "Elegy on John Hogg"

Fergusson's next production, dated by the poet, "*Sept.* 18," appeared in *The Weekly Magazine* on September 23, just one week after "The Election." Another comic elegy, this poem, entitled "Elegy on John Hogg, late Porter to the University of St Andrews," is a nostalgic tribute to the eccentric old porter, John Hogg, who was one of the college "characters" during

Fergusson's time at St. Andrews. Like the earlier "Elegy on Gregory," it is in the pure tradition of Robert Sempill's "Habbie Simson" as it was handed down to Fergusson through Hamilton of Gilbertfield and Allan Ramsay; but, unlike the "Gregory," this elegy does not appear to be specifically indebted to any of these earlier writers in the genre. The originality of the poem, its accomplished craftsmanship, and its strongly personal flavor, when contrasted with the imitative technique and immature though spirited treatment of the "Elegy on Gregory," are evidence of how much Fergusson had matured as a poet since his apprentice days at St. Andrews. Incidentally, the opening stanza of the "Elegy on Hogg," with its familiar joking address to Death and its comical "licket-pricket-tricket-wicket" rimes, seems to have made a lasting impression on Burns and stuck in his subconscious memory, since traces of its influence occur in two of his poems, widely separated in dates of composition—in "Death and Doctor Hornbook" (1785) and in the fourth stanza of "Verses to Collector Mitchell" (1795).

Fergusson's elegy is interesting in content both for its precise and charming character sketch of John Hogg and for the incidental insights it gives into Fergusson's own experience at St. Andrews. It is one of the very few poems in which Fergusson tells us something about himself. The elegy is simply and effectively organized to show in how many and various ways the students will miss their old friend, John Hogg, always a favorite with them. Fergusson presents the details of the poem in a clearly defined structural order, describing first Hogg's knowingness in advising students and professors, then his quaint and sententious manner of rousing the students in the morning and his habit of quoting the proverbs of Solomon, his sociability with the students, and, finally, his parsimony. By lighting up these contrasting sides of Hogg's character, Fergusson succeeds in giving a remarkably full and sharp impression of the whole man.

In his opening stanzas, Fergusson imagines the shattering blow to the University occasioned by the old porter's death, with "Kate Kennedy," a bell in the college steeple, tolling his knell. Here he uses the same kind of comic exaggeration that we have noted in the "Elegy on Gregory," this method being, in fact, traditional in the comic elegy genre.

Now ilka glaikit scholar lown   silly; fellow
May dander wae wi' *duddy gown;*   stroll woefully; ragged
KATE KENNEDY to dowy crune   sad tolling
May mourn and clink,
And steeples o' Saint Andrew's town
To yird may sink.   earth

In stanzas 6 and 7, Fergusson gives us his vivid and humorous memories of being awakened in the morning after one of his escapades by "Johnny," whose duty it was to rouse the students early every day:

Ah, Johnny! aften did I grumble
Frae cozy bed fu' ear' to tumble;   early
Whan art and part I'd been in some ill,
Troth I was sweer,   reluctant
His words they brodit like a wumill   pricked; gimlet
Frae ear to ear.

Whan I had been fu' laith to rise,   loath
John than begude to moralize: then began
"The TITHER NAP, the SLUGGARD cries,   other
"And turns him round;
"Sae spake auld Solomon the wise,
"Divine profound!"

The sententious old porter was apparently noted for his partiality for Solomon, besides being, like many eighteenth-century Scots in humble life, an authority on the Bible in general:

Nae dominie, or wise mess John,   teacher; minister
Was better lear'd in Solomon;   learned
He cited proverbs one by one . . .

In stanzas 9 and 10 we find that John, far from being a Deist, preferred the old-fashioned literal interpretation of the Scriptures. He will have nothing to do with new-fangled theories about the rotation of the earth. Such attitudes are, of course, perfectly typical of the stanch, unbending type of old-fashioned Presbyterian of Fergusson's day, the type immortalized by Scott in *The Heart of Midlothian* in the character of Davie Deans. These stanzas on John's belligerent theology help to characterize him, to fill out Fergusson's fine picture of the man.

In his next two stanzas, Fergusson recalls with touching

nostalgia the many cozy, sociable evenings he had spent with a few friends in the porter's hospitable lodge:

Say ye, *red gowns*! that aften here	students
Hae toasted bakes to *Kattie*'s beer,	biscuits
Gin 'ere thir days hae had their peer,	if; those
Sae blyth, sae daft;	
You'll ne'er again in life's career	
Sit ha'f sae saft.	half

These wistful lines take on added poignancy in the light of Fergusson's own tragically brief and unfulfilled career, when we consider that he had but four months of active life left to him when he wrote them. Well might he look back on those carefree college days as the happiest time of his life, for he was in fact destined never again to "sit ha'f sae saft."

He returns in his last four stanzas to further memories of old John Hogg, reflecting whimsically on the porter's notorious thrift. To save money John limited himself, we are told in the brilliant thirteenth stanza, to one shave a week:

Wi' haffit locks, sae smooth and sleek,	cheek
John look'd like ony antient Greek;	
He was a Nazarene a' the week,	
And doughtna tell out	would not
A bawbee Scots to straik his cheek	halfpenny; stroke
Till Sunday fell out.	

For John ay lo'ed to turn the pence,	loved
Thought poortith was a great offence . . .	poverty

Fergusson develops his penetrative and amusing study of Hogg's materialistic point of view in the next stanzas, and ends his poem with ironic praise of John's penurious habits. The satire here, as in the rest of the poem, is thoroughly good-natured and void of malice. Fergusson concentrates on Hogg's eccentricities, but at the same time he manages to suggest that the old porter was essentially a good and worthy man for whom he has sincere regard and a kind of nostalgic affection. In this respect, the poem is typical of Fergusson's comprehensive realism, his sane and balanced vision. He does not allow Hogg's eccentricities to blind him to the man's essential worthiness, but his warm sentiment toward the porter is modified by his incisive, but good-natured, mockery of Hogg's shortcomings. This balance between intellect and emotion is a fundamental feature of Fergusson's realism, and it becomes increasingly evident in his later work.

On the whole, the "Elegy on Hogg" is, as David Daiches remarks, "perhaps the most brilliant . . . of all the mock elegies in the 'Habbie Simson' tradition."[5] Certainly the poem reveals Fergusson's developing ability to portray character, his keen observation, his surprisingly mature and shrewd insight, and, finally, his accomplished poetic technique. Taking a person of no special account in the world as his subject, Fergusson creates for us an entertaining and profoundly human portrait, once again anticipating Burns and, ultimately, Wordsworth in their poems about "common" people. Much of the charm of the elegy lies in its highly personal, familiar tone, filled as it is with Fergusson's tender and nostalgic memories of those carefree, hopeful years at St. Andrews. An unspectacular work, full of quiet, insinuative humor, the "Elegy on Hogg" is one of Fergusson's most consistently successful vernacular poems.

V "Dumfries"

Fergusson's next poem resulted from an extended excursion he took in the last week of September, 1773, during his vacation from the Commissary Office. Accompanied by a friend, one Lieutenant Wilson, R. N., he walked from Edinburgh to Dumfries (about eighty miles), where he visited Charles Salmon, a fellow poet, formerly of Edinburgh. Fergusson's reputation had preceded him to Nithsdale; he was welcomed enthusiastically and showered with flattering attention by admirers in the Dumfries area. On his departure he composed, more or less extemporaneously, his poem "Dumfries." Grosart erroneously states that these verses were first published in the *Lives of Scottish Poets* (London, 1822);[6] actually, they originally appeared immediately after their composition in the *Dumfries Weekly Magazine* (III, 94), signed and dated by the author: "R. Fergusson. Sept. 26."[7]

From an artistic point of view, "Dumfries" is of very minor importance. The poem is an occasional piece, slight in content (it is a tribute to the natural beauties of Nithsdale), thrown off hurriedly without Fergusson's usually careful attention to form, but it does show something of his characteristic vigor of expression. In stanzas 5 and 6, for example, Fergusson imagines Horace—"that pleasant sinner, / That loo'd gude wine to synd [wash down] his dinner"—migrating to Nithsdale to enjoy the fine claret there. And in his final stanza he rather wistfully pictures himself in the Horatian role, as a country gentleman in Nithsdale:

O Jove, man, gie's some orrow pence,	spare
Mair siller, an' a wie mair sense,	money
I'd big to you a rural spence,	build; country parlor
An' bide a' simmer,	
An' cald frae saul and body fence	
With frequent brimmer.	

Burns was to share with Fergusson this Horatian ideal, never realized by either poet, this dream of someday living a retired life of literary leisure in the country.

This poem, finally, was written at the request of Fergusson's admirers around Dumfries; and the fact is significant as proof that by 1773 Fergusson had beyond doubt attained the stature and reputation of a truly national poet. His work was being read with enthusiasm not only in Edinburgh itself, but in far away provincial towns like Dumfries. We have already noted evidences of his popularity in the widely separated districts of Berwickshire and Perthshire, and now Dumfriesshire, facts which prove that by 1773 Fergusson was no longer merely the poet of Edinburgh: he had become, in a real sense, the poet of Scotland.

VI "The Sitting of the Session"

On November 4, Fergusson's "The Sitting of the Session," a companion piece to the earlier "Rising of the Session," appeared in *The Weekly Magazine*. The poem was written expressly for the occasion, the opening of the Court of Session for the winter term which took place on November 12. It describes the return of prosperity caused by this event among the lawyers and hangers-on of the legal profession. The poem shows some similarity in theme, especially in the last few stanzas, to Dunbar's "Tidings frae the Session," a work that Fergusson could have found in Walter Ruddiman's *Choice Collection* (1766);[8] Fergusson's first two lines, setting the season of the year, may have given Burns suggestions for the opening stanza of "A Winter Night."

"The Sitting of the Session" is very similar in theme, descriptive method, and style to its predecessor, "The Rising of the Session," though it contains a sharper critcism of the ways of the law than does the earlier poem. Two or three quotations will illustrate its flavor. After his first stanza, which fixes the season of the year, Fergusson comments (stanzas 2 and 3) on how the sitting of the Session stimulates business in Edinburgh. His third stanza typifies the clever, imaginative style of this poem:

The COURT O' SESSION, weel wat I,	know
Pitts ilk chiel's *whittle* i' the pye,	every fellow's knife
Can criesh the slaw-gaun wheels whan dry,	grease; slow-going
Till Session's done,	
Tho' they'll gi'e mony a cheep and cry	
Or twalt o' June.	ere twelfth

The Court closed for the winter session in Fergusson's time early in March to reconvene for the summer session on June 12; thus, the poet looks forward in this stanza to the "vacance time" between sessions when the wheels of business will give "mony a cheep and cry" for want of lubrication. The idea of lubrication leads him to consider the heavy drinking that inevitably went with the occasion. The taverns in the "Outer House" begin to operate at full blast as soon as the session opens. In stanza 5 we catch another vivid glimpse of Robin Gibb, the tavern keeper whom Fergusson had characterized so brilliantly in "The Rising":

ROB GIBB's grey gizz, new frizzl'd fine,	wig
Will white as ony snaw-ba' shine;	snowball
Weel does he lo'e the LAWEN coin	love; reckoning
Whan dossied down,	tossed
For whisky gills or dribbs of wine	drops
In cauld forenoon.	

This stanza, with its highly effective alliteration and satiric overtones, is superbly executed. Fergusson's use of the verb "dossied down" is especially graphic and suggestive: this strongly idiomatic expression is very precise in its connotations; it means "to fling down in a rough, careless manner," and is, therefore, extremely appropriate in describing the way in which Robin Gibb's customers flip their coins on the counter when ordering drinks.

In his last four stanzas, Fergusson portrays with biting satire the operations of the cumbersome legal machinery in Edinburgh during this busy period when

The LAWYER's *skelfs,* and PRINTER's *presses,*	shelves
Grain unco sair wi' weighty cases . . .	groan very sorely

He attacks not only the greed and unscrupulousness of the lawyers, but also the utter folly of ignorant people who have recourse to law in settling minor disputes. And the fantastic complexity and delay of the law itself are exposed in Fergusson's brilliant final stanza:

But LAW's a DRAW-WELL unco deep,	remarkably
Withouten RIM fock out to keep;	
A donnart chiel, whan drunk, may dreep	stupid; drop
Fu' sleely in,	easily
But finds the gate baith *stay* and *steep,*	way; steep
'Ere out he win.	

"The Sitting of the Session" is, on the whole, a more successful poem than its companion piece. It is more unified, more single-minded in purpose, more direct and powerful in its satiric method, and more mature in its penetrative insight into the total situation. Fergusson is not content merely to describe the scene in its lively outward manifestations: he penetrates beneath the surface of the frenzied activities at the Court of Session to reflect on the serious meaning which these activities hold for society in general. Though humorous and vivacious in tone, his poem is forthright, dramatic criticism of the whole legal system as it existed in his day, a system with which he was thoroughly familiar. Thus, although it is not one of his major works, "The Sitting of the Session" is very significant in showing that Fergusson's poetry was steadily increasing in depth and maturity, and that Fergusson himself was rapidly developing into a powerful and perceptive satiric poet. His economy of expression is here, as elsewhere, remarkable, his technique excellent; but the most striking characteristic of the poem is his maturity of treatment.

VII "A Drink Eclogue"

Fergusson's last poem in the eclogue form, entitled "A Drink Eclogue," appeared in Ruddiman's magazine just one week after "The Sitting of the Session," on November 11. Written in heroic couplets and similar in method to "Plainstanes and Causey," it presents a debate or "flyting" between two imaginary characters, a bottle of brandy and a bottle of whisky in a tavern cellar, with a third character, the "Landlady," coming in at the end to arbitrate the dispute. Thus the poem is another "flyting eclogue," the poetic form created by Fergusson in "Plainstanes and Causey" by combining the old Scottish "flyting" genre with the pastoral eclogue. In theme, "A Drink Eclogue" is reminiscent of "Hame Content," combining social satire with intensely nationalistic feeling. The two characters, Brandy and Whisky, are portrayed as sharply contrasted human types, while at the same time they symbolize opposing social forces: Whisky stands for the old-fashioned Scottish way of life, the distinctive national culture, whereas Brandy represents the enfeebling influence of foreign innovations which were threatening the ancient cultural identity of Scotland. Fergusson's sympathies are, of course, all with Whisky. He portrays Brandy as a vain and frivolous aristocrat, an effeminate braggart; Whisky, on the other hand, is a man of the people, an honest, sturdy Scot with all the distinctive national virtues. It will be noted that at the end of the poem, when the Landlady arrives to settle the debate, Brandy is exposed as a fraud after all, a "mongrel loun," and not the genuine article. This brilliant ironic twist reinforces the symbolic meaning of the poem: Scots who affect foreign manners and fashions remain Scots at heart; the thin veneer of foreign culture which they take such pains to acquire is unbecoming to them and proves to be in the end nothing more than a ridiculous, vain, enfeebling affectation.

"A Drink Eclogue" is as boldly original in its conception as "Plainstanes and Causey." As in "An Eclogue," "Plainstanes and Causey," and "The Ghaists," Fergusson was again breaking the ground for the vernacular duologues of Burns. In both theme and method it anticipates "The Twa Dogs" in particular, in which Burns follows Fergusson's thematic development very closely, beginning with a skillful, matter-of-fact introduction describing the two speakers, and gradually turning their conversation into a brilliant social satire on precisely the same themes. Burns's "Scotch Drink" (especially stanzas 15 and 16) is also, and even more obviously, indebted to "A Drink Eclogue."

The imaginative force of the poem is well illustrated in the opening lines in which Fergusson ingeniously establishes the temperamental motives for the "flyting" that follows by explaining that the two bottles (Brandy and Whisky) "Grew canker'd; for the twa war het within, / An' het-skin'd fock to flyting soon begin." Brandy opens the argument with a magnificent bit of bravado:

Black be your fa! ye cottar loun mislear'd,	fall; uncouth
Blawn by the PORTERS, *chairmen,* CITY-GUARD;	drunk
Ha'e ye nae breeding, that you shaw your nose	
Anent my sweetly gusted cordial dose.	side by side with
I've been near pauky courts, and aften there	artful
Ha'e ca'd HYSTERICKS frae the dowy fair . . .	driven; gloomy

Fergusson's style in these lines and, in fact, throughout the eclogue is full of vigor and is highly dramatic. Brandy's absurd boast of having "ca'd HYSTERICKS frae the dowy fair" is a fine touch, suggesting as it does his vain, frivolous character. Whisky's reaction throughout to Brandy's snobbish attitude and ridiculous pretensions is restrained and sensible. He refuses to get excited over Brandy's blustering, but continues to drive home his own point of view with persistent and sober logic. Fergusson shows notable artistic control and imaginative insight in his portrayal of Whisky: for example, he makes him ignore Brandy's empty threat of violence ("Gif [if] honour wad but lat, a CHALLENGE shou'd / Twin [rob] ye o' Highland TONGUE and Highland BLUDE") as though he considered such a threat, coming from such a person, as beneath contempt.

The theme of Whisky's arguments is, significantly, nationalistic. He resents the fashionable craze for drinking brandy, a phenomenon which had increased alarmingly since the Union, until, as Whisky points out, even the Highland chairmen of Edinburgh have taken to drinking champagne and other French liquors. He comments shrewdly on the fact that whereas in France brandy is considered a common drink and is ordinarily consumed by "*sarkless* [shirtless] soldiers," in Scotland it is worshipped as the most aristocratic and fashionable of beverages simply because it is foreign and expensive. The country lairds and "greedy Bankers" of the city are willing to strip their estates and sell their souls for brandy; meanwhile, the traditional Scottish drink, whisky, which is cheap and plentiful, stands neglected on the shelves:

. . . tho' I can heat the skin,	
And set the saul upon a merry pin,	
Yet I am hameil, there's the sour mischance!	home-bred
I'm no frae Turkey, Italy, or France;	
For now our Gentles gabbs are grown sae nice,	mouths
At thee they toot, an' never speer my price . . .	drink; ask

Brandy disdainfully associates Whisky with poverty-stricken poets:

Frae some poor poet, o'er as poor a pot,	
Ye've lear'd to crack sae crouse, ye haveril Scot!	learned; talk; boldly; prating

Far from being ashamed, Whisky is proud of the fact that he has inspired Scotland's finest and most patriotic poets, and he pays a tribute to Allan Ramsay, the whisky-drinking bard of the people, whose songs are on everyone's tongue.

At this point, Brandy calls upon the Landlady to give the final verdict and end the debate. The Landlady's vigorous speech exposing Brandy as a fraud is perhaps the most brilliant stroke in the eclogue, and it forms the perfect conclusion:

Will you your breeding threep, ye *mongrel loun!*	assert, boast about
Frae hame-bred liquor dy'd to colour brown?	
So FLUNKY braw, whan drest in master's claise,	fine; clothes
Struts to Auld Reikie's cross on sunny days,	
Till some auld comerade, ablins out o' place,	maybe
Near the vain upstart shaws his meagre face;	
Bumbaz'd he loups frae sight, and jooks his ken,	taken aback; leaps; dodges
Fley'd to be seen amang the tassel'd train.	afraid

This final comparison of the false brandy with the "flunky braw" is effective in driving home Fergusson's message. The whole apparatus of the debate between Brandy and Whisky is, in fact, an ingenious device used by Fergusson to present in concrete form his theme of social criticism.

In "A Drink Eclogue," Fergusson attacks the same kind of social affectation and sham which he had satirized in "Braid Claith," "Plainstanes and Causey," "Butterfly," "Hame Content," "To the Principal and Professors," and in two or three of his English poems, notably "Fashion." His attitude toward the mores of his time is clearly conservative. He feels that his countrymen are tending more and more to follow strange gods, and in so doing are gradually undermining and destroying the hard-won integrity and traditions of their national life. In his poetry Fergusson is trying to check this tendency toward disintegration; to persuade men to turn back to the old-fashioned, homely Scottish virtues; to develop their own national culture; and to appreciate their own resources. Fergusson's spirit, like Burns's, is the proud, heroic spirit of Scottish independence; and all his vernacular poetry represents, in a sense, a confession of faith in Scotland, in the vitality of her people, language, and culture. This spirit of genuine patriotism is nowhere more evident than in "A Drink Eclogue."

From a purely artistic point of view, Fergusson's last eclogue is excellent, and it ranks with "An Eclogue" and "Plainstanes and Causey" as one of his most successful efforts in this form. The dialogue is amusing, spirited, and dramatic; the fantasy is well sustained, yet never conflicts with the development of the underlying satiric purpose of the poem. Fergusson manages his couplets with a high degree of technical skill, so that the rigid metrical form does not inhibit his natural, conversational style. Though not one of his most spectacular pieces, the eclogue stands high among Fergusson's Scottish poems, and gives further evidence of his steadily increasing maturity as a sensitive and conscientious writer on serious themes.

VIII "To My Auld Breeks"

On November 25, 1773, appeared Fergusson's last Scottish poem ever to be published in *The Weekly Magazine:* the delightful address "To My Auld Breeks," the most intimately personal of all Fergusson's works. In this poem, written in tetrameter couplets, Fergusson makes whimsical fun of his own poverty, the common fate of poets, as he bids a regretful farewell to his old friend, a pair of worn-out "breeks." There is no hint of disgruntled complaint or rebellion in these lines; rather, the prevailing mood is one of humorous reflection mingled in some passages with a certain wistfulness, and it is only lightly touched with general satire on the ways of the world. There is, incidentally, a clever passage in John Phillips' "The Splendid Shilling" [9] concerning the author's torn trousers ("My *Galligaskins*") which may well have provided the initial stimulus to Fergusson's imagination, but the resulting poem is all his own and bears the unmistakable imprint of his poetic personality. "To My Auld Breeks," as might be expected, made its mark on Burns, who seized upon one of Fergusson's happiest metaphors ("Wi' you I've speel'd the braes o' rime") and adapted it to his own purposes in his "To William Simpson," where it crops up, significantly, in a stanza devoted to praise of the Scottish poets, including Fergusson himself.

In this charming poem Fergusson personifies his "breeks," imagining how they must feel at being cast off after so long and intimate an association with the poet. In the first part of his address he tries to explain to his breeks why they must part: he has patched and mended them until they are beyond redemption. At this point he pictures his old breeks wagging their "duds" (rags) at him indignantly at this callous abandonment:

You needna wag your DUDS o' clouts,	rags of patches
Nor fa' into your dorty pouts,	pettish, sullen
To think that erst you've hain'd my TAIL	shielded
Frae WIND and WEET, frae SNAW and HAIL,	wet
And for reward, whan bald and hummil,	shabby
Frae garret high to dree a tumble.	suffer

This is grand fun; what follows is even better. Fergusson points out that he does not wish to cast off his old friend; he would keep his breeks if he could, but he is forced to part with them out of sheer economic necessity. The pockets are so full of holes that whenever he wears the breeks he is in danger of losing the few miserable coins he possesses:

Now to befriend, it wad be folly,	
Your raggit hide an' pouches holey;	pockets

For wha but kens a poet's placks — copper coins
Get mony weary flaws an' cracks,
And canna thole to hae them tint, — endure; lost
As he sae seenil sees the mint? — seldom

But the fate of the poor old worn-out breeks is a common one in this world of selfishness and parasitism.

In the second section of the poem Fergusson commiserates with the breeks and recalls with touching nostalgia some of the good and bad times they have gone through together. These lines are of considerable biographical interest, for they give us brief insights into some of Fergusson's attitudes and experiences on the best possible authority, the poet himself:

Yet gratefu' hearts, to make amends,
Will ay be sorry for their friends,
And I for thee—As mony a time
Wi' you I've speel'd the braes o' rime, — climbed
Whare for the time the Muse ne'er cares
For siller, or sic guilefu' wares . . . — money; such

. . . .

You've seen me round the bickers reel — drinking bowls
Wi' heart as hale as temper'd steel,
And face sae apen, free and blyth, — open
Nor thought that sorrow there cou'd kyth; — show
But the niest manent this was lost, — next
Like gowan in December's frost. — daisy

Here the phrase, "the Muse ne'er cares for siller," tends to confirm the belief that Fergusson did not look upon himself as a sort of literary hack spinning out his rimes to pick up a few shillings, but conceived himself as a poet in a truer and nobler sense: as a dedicated spirit who writes because he has something to say which he feels compelled to express in poetic form. The dreary job in the Commissary Office was necessary to keep body and soul together; but his real life was with the "Muse" in the exuberant world of his poetic imagination. While writing his poems, he could "for the time" forget the bitterness, the frustration of his career, and his hard, endless struggle for the bare necessities of subsistence. The latter part of the passage cited above is tragically prophetic. The tremendous strain under which Fergusson was working had evidently taken its toll, so that already he was subject to sudden fits of melancholia in the midst of his gayest and most triumphant moods. These lines seem to convey a premonition of disaster, but Fergusson probably never suspected when he wrote them that he was going to collapse within a matter of weeks.

These reflections on himself, however, cast only a light and momentary shadow over the generally sunny atmosphere of the poem. In his next verse paragraph Fergusson shifts attention promptly back to the breeks. He declares that if "*Prick-the-louse*" —the tailor—could mend his trousers he would continue to wear them in spite of the fact that they have gone out of fashion; but unfortunately they are beyond repairing. At this point Fergusson introduces a touch of sly satire ingeniously expressed in macaronic verse. The cleverness of his rimes is perfectly suited to the light satiric tone of the poem as a whole:

But, hegh! the times *vicissitudo,*	
Gars ither breeks decay as you do.	makes
Thae MACARONIES, braw and windy,	these
Maun fail—*Sic transit gloria mundi*!	must

It may be noted that the Scots pronunciation of "windy" as "wundy" makes the rime with "*mundi*" almost identical. Fergusson imagines what will become of his old breeks after he throws them out. Perhaps they will end up in "some madam's chaumer" to be made into female underwear, or perhaps—and this is one of the finest imaginative strokes in the poem—they will become a ghost to haunt some poet who has unaccountably grown rich, to remind him of his earlier poverty:

Glowr in his face, like spectre gaunt,	
Remind him o' his former want,	
To cow his daffin and his pleasure,	daunt; fun
And gar him live within the measure.	make

After a brief reference to the way in which Philip of Macedonia kept his humility, Fergusson ends his poem on this note of wry humor.

"To My Auld Breeks" is unquestionably one of the most charming and distinctive of Fergusson's poems. Once more his subject matter is unusual, not to say revolutionary, for his time; he manages to make delightful fantasy and penetrating poetic satire out of the most unpromising of materials—an old, tattered pair of trousers. His ability to do so in this piece—and in others such as "Caller Oysters," "Braid Claith," and "Plainstanes and Causey"—is positive proof that he possessed imaginative powers of a high order.

The distinctiveness of the poem lies not only in its subject but in Fergusson's treatment of it. "To My Auld Breeks" is intensely personal and intimate in style; Fergusson is speaking openly and directly to the reader about his own problems and feelings. In this respect the poem is unique among Fergusson's works: never before had he dared to bring himself as an individual human being so clearly into the foreground. In so doing he provided Burns with a precedent for his many self-revealing, highly personalized poems. This subjective quality in "To My Auld Breeks" is important from another point of view: it shows that Fergusson was becoming aware of himself as a literary personality; he had discovered that he could write interesting and meaningful poems about himself, as well as about other people. Accordingly, he turns from his brilliant objective descriptions of Hallow Fair and Leith Races to write a delightful poem on Rob Fergusson and his breeks. It is perhaps not too rash to conjecture that, given time to develop, his poetry would have acquired the powerful personal magnetism that characterizes the works of Burns. At any rate, "To My Auld Breeks" is the best evidence we have that Fergusson was definitely moving in that direction and was rapidly approaching emotional and artistic maturity.

IX *Two Songs*

We now come to a final group of three Scottish poems, comprising two songs, "The Lea-Rig" and "Hallowfair," and a long descriptive poem in tetrameter couplets, "Auld Reikie," none of which can be accurately dated since they did not appear in *The Weekly Magazine* nor in Fergusson's 1773 volume; but all three poems were probably written sometime during 1773. The "Lea-Rig" was first published in a song-book, *The Charmer* (Edinburgh, 1782), and then again in the first volume of James Johnson's *Scots Musical Museum* (Edinburgh, 1787). The song was ascribed to Fergusson by Burns himself in a note on the *Museum* version which he asserts was written "by poor Fergusson in one of his merry humours." [10] In the same note, Burns records a fragment of a much older song of unknown authorship, beginning "I'll rowe thee o'er the lea-rig, / My ain kind deary, O." Both Fergusson and Burns (in his treatment of the same theme, "When o'er the hill the eastern star") worked from this ancient model, each incorporating the refrain, "My ain kind deary, O," and the traditional tune.

Of the three renderings of this "Lea-Rig" theme, however, Burns's is unquestionably the best. But Fergusson's, too, is good. His verses are lively enough, with fresh pastoral imagery which is well suited to the original idea of the song and genuinely lyrical feeling. His "Lea-Rig" is, of course, a slight performance, for, when judged absolutely as literature, it gives the impression of an experimental exercise. But the song is of some significance as being probably Fergusson's first attempt at Scottish song writing. Though only moderately successful, "Lea-Rig" gives further evidence of Fergusson's growing confidence in himself, of his tendency (especially marked during 1773) to branch out—to broaden and diversify his poetic activity, and to try his hand at new forms and genres.

While "The Lea-Rig" is almost certainly Fergusson's, the authorship of "Hallowfair," the other song attributed to him, is much more open to question. David Herd, a friend of Fergusson and a fellow "knight" of the Cape Club, was the first to print the song (anonymously) in his *Ancient and Modern Scottish Songs* (Edinburgh, 1776). It appeared again in James Johnson's *Scots Musical Museum* (Part V, Edinburgh, 1797) where, for the first time, it was ascribed to Fergusson by Johnson.[11] But David Irving, the biographer of Fergusson, and, more recently, George Eyre-Todd, attribute the song to Francis Sempill of Beltrees (?1616-1685), son of the author of "Habbie Simson."[12] On the whole, however, Fergusson's claim to "Hallowfair" seems the stronger, and we could attribute it to him with a reasonable degree of certainty if it were written in his characteristic style; but unfortunately it is not. The song has a definitely old-fashioned flavor for Fergusson's time, and it lacks his careful craftsmanship. In view of the slender evidence available, the best guess would be that "Hallowfair" is an older folk song partially reworked by Fergusson for his friend Herd's anthology. At any rate, "Hallowfair" is obviously modeled on the lively seventeenth-century song, "The Blythsome Bridal," being set to the same tune and written in the same distinctive eight-line stanza. It also shows a strong resemblance in certain details to a song entitled "Muirland Willie," which appeared in William Thomson's early collection *Orpheus Caledonius* (1733).[13] "Muirland Willie," too, is in the tradition of "The Blythsome Bridal," and all three songs are more or less akin to the "Christis Kirk" genre.

"Hallowfair," a lively, vigorous piece, describes the antics of a group of rustics who are driving their live-stock through Edinburgh on their way to the Hallow Fair held on the outskirts. The song suffers chiefly from lack of logical arrangement and coherence. It is haphazardly constructed; and, though most of the individual parts are effective in themselves, little attempt is made to link them, to have one incident develop out of the one preceding. This general looseness can be illustrated in a brief quotation from stanza 2:

But MAGGIE was wondrous jealous
  To see WILLIE busked sae braw; — dressed; finely
And SAWNEY he sat in the alehouse,
  And hard at the liquor did caw. — drive

In the lines immediately preceding this passage, the poet describes Maggie and Willie; then here, without any pause or transition, he introduces an entirely new character, "Sawney," who apparently has nothing to do with Maggie or Willie. This lack of coherence in the song seemingly argues against Fergusson's authorship. On the other hand, one section of the poem, stanzas 3, 4, and 5, describing the misadventures of Wattie "the muirland laddie," is brilliantly written, with a verve, a sly satiric touch, and an economy of expression which suggest Fergusson's descriptive style. If Fergusson had anything to do with this song, these traces of unevenness in performance indicate that he acted as a reviser of a much older and cruder work, touching it up here and there and perhaps filling it out with stanzas of his own composition.

In the final analysis, however, it is doubtful that Fergusson's natural bent was in the direction of song writing, judging from the bulk of his extant poetry. Though his work as a whole is not lacking in emotional value, his mind shows a strongly intellectual cast, and his poetic imagination is primarily a satiric imagination, which makes it seem unlikely that he could ever have excelled in the expression of lyrical emotion. There is no hint in his poetry of the kind of spontaneous lyric urge and intuition that characterizes the work of Burns, who began his poetical career as a writer of songs. "The Lea-Rig," for example, though a thoroughly competent performance, shows nothing of the splendid power of some of Burns's early songs, such as "Mary Morison."

X "Auld Reikie"

In "Auld Reikie," by far Fergusson's longest and certainly one of his most impressive poems, the poet turned again to the tetrameter couplet and to his favorite subject matter—the everyday life and social manners of Old Edinburgh. The poem was printed separately in 1773, "for the author," in a slim pamphlet, with a dedication to Sir William Forbes in some of the copies and with the subtitle, "Canto I," which suggests that further installments were to follow. The original design was never completed, however, presumably because Fergusson met with no encouragement from Sir William Forbes. After publication of his first "Canto," the poet merely added a few lines to round off the poem, and it was reprinted in its final form with the additions five years after Fergusson's death in Part II of the 1779 volume.

"Auld Reikie" is an extraordinary poem from several points of view. The basic concept is in itself daring and unusual: Fergusson attempts, with notable success, to recreate the flavor, the atmosphere, the very life of a whole city in all its multifarious activities, its changing moods, its roaring noises, its colors, smells, and bustling motion—to capture and to give it meaning and permanence by expressing it in terms of poetic art. There is nothing at all like this poem in earlier Scottish literature; and in English poetry up to Fergusson's time the only work that I know of which is comparable in scope to "Auld Reikie" is John Gay's "Trivia."

There is good reason to believe, indeed, that the original idea for "Auld Reikie" came from Gay's poem, that Fergusson was here attempting to do for Edinburgh something on the order of what Gay had already done for London, with perhaps some additional suggestions from Swift's "Description of the Morning" and "Description of a City Shower" and other such pieces. A few of Fergusson's details may also have been directly inspired by Gay: the passage in "Auld Reikie" on the insincerity and vanity of elaborate funerals (lines 163 ff.), for example, is very similar to "Trivia," III, 225 ff. On the other hand, the two poems obviously differ sharply both in style and structural method. "Auld Reikie" is no servile imitation of Gay, but a remarkably fresh and original work written with Fergusson's customary vigor in his distinctively personal and attractive style.

Like most of Fergusson's better poems, "Auld Reikie" made its mark on Burns, who seems to be recalling it in two or three places. Fergusson's attack on religious hypocrisy (lines 231 ff.), for example, probably suggested Burns's passages in "Epistle to a Young Friend" (stanza 9) and in "The Brigs of Ayr" (lines 146-7); and it doubtless influenced his satiric treatments of the same theme in the "Address to the Unco Guid," "Holy Willie's Prayer," "The Holy Fair," and other poems.

"Auld Reikie" can be divided structurally into two halves, the first of which contains some sixteen verse paragraphs, and is neatly organized, after an introduction, in terms of morning, afternoon, and evening scenes (paragraphs 3-5, 6, 7-16). At the end of the sixteenth verse paragraph, however, there is an abrupt break in the smooth development of the poem. At this point Fergusson abandons his morning-afternoon-evening scheme, and he turns to treatment of other aspects of Edinburgh life which do not fit into this pattern. The second half of the poem falls into five groups of paragraphs on the following topics: contrasted description of the attractive vegetable market and the repulsive meat market (17-20); Sunday in Edinburgh (21-23); Holyroodhouse and poverty (24-26); contrast between George Drummond, late Lord Provost of Edinburgh and benefactor of the poor, and the present corrupt civic leaders (27); concluding eulogy on Edinburgh (28-29). The three central sections of the second half of the poem—on Edinburgh Sundays, on Holyrood and poverty, and on the city government (paragraphs 21-23, 24-26, and 27)—are ingeniously linked, one developing naturally out of the other. The section on the markets (paragraphs 17-20), however, is the weakest part of the poem from a structural point of view, being more or less unrelated to what precedes and follows it. Thus, although "Auld Reikie" contains long passages which are carefully organized around related themes and linked by smooth transitions, the poem as a whole suffers from the lack of overall design. There is no single structural principle to give unity and direction to all of the parts; and, as a result, the poem gives an impression of looseness.

But whatever "Auld Reikie" lacks in firmness of structure is amply compensated for by the brilliant artistry of individual passages. In a poem of this length it is, of course, manifestly impractical to attempt to treat all of the noteworthy passages and lines in detail, but a few typical examples will be enough perhaps to illustrate the important features of Fergusson's style and method. He opens, appropriately, with a rousing salute to Edinburgh:

AULD REIKIE, wale o' ilka Town	best; every
That SCOTLAND kens beneath the Moon;	
Where couthy Chiels at E'ening meet	sociable fellows
Their bizzing CRAIGS and MOUS to weet;	parched throats
And blythly gar auld Care gae bye	make
Wi' blinkit and wi' bleering Eye . . .	

These lines are notable for their warmth and vigor, expressing as they do Fergusson's hearty and unchanging love for the old grey city. It is significant that he begins his poem with this reference to drinking, always a dominant feature of Edinburgh social life in his time.

The next section of the poem, on morning scenes, begins with a splendid couplet portraying sunrise over the city, followed by lines describing the early activities of housemaids and the foul morning smells of sewage (which Fergusson whimsically refers to as "EDINA's Roses"). This passage is photographic in its terse and impressive realism, as the following extracts show:

Now Morn, with bonny Purpie-smiles,	purple
Kisses the Air-cock o' St. Giles;	weathervane
Rakin their Ein, the Servant Lasses	rubbing; eyes
Early begin their Lies and Clashes . . .	gossip
. . . .	
On Stair wi' TUB, or PAT in hand,	pot
The Barefoot HOUSEMAIDS looe to stand,	love
That antrin Fock may ken how SNELL	strangers; strong
Auld Reikie will at MORNING SMELL.	

This passage is typical of Fergusson's comprehensive realism: he does not allow his profound affection for Auld Reekie to blind him to the city's more obnoxious characteristics; yet, at the same time, his description of the foul smells and of the sordid side of Edinburgh social life and customs is softened and modified by his emotional response to the unique beauty of this grimy old city, a beauty which co-exists with its squalor. This balance, this double vision, distinguishes Fergusson's style in "Auld Reikie" from that of Swift in his fiercely realistic satires on London life. Fergusson perceives that the unique atmosphere, the essence of old Edinburgh, lies in the startling and unusual contrasts, both physical and social, which the city presents; and he re-creates that atmosphere, with remarkable precision and intimacy, in terms of these contrasts. This double vision, reconciling beauty and ugliness, and unifying thought and feeling so that each modifies the other, is ever present in "Auld Reikie" and is the basic artistic principle of the poem. This principle is clearly discernible in the lines quoted above in which Fergusson, in a single charming couplet, suggests the fragile, fleeting loveliness of sunrise over the ancient spire of St. Giles, and follows it immediately with lines about the slovenly housemaids and the nauseous morning smells of the city.

The section on Edinburgh night life, in which Fergusson portrays in sharp, vivid detail typical characters and scenes of the city after dark, is perhaps the most brilliantly executed part of the poem. The passage describing the belligerent ramble of a drunken "Bruiser" or pugilist is worth noting as a fine example of Fergusson's descriptive method. It begins as follows:

FRAE joyous Tavern, reeling drunk,	
Wi' fiery Phizz, and Ein half sunk,	face; eyes
Behad the Bruiser, Fae to a'	behold; foe
That in the reek o' Gardies fa':	reach; arms fall
Close by his Side, a feckless Race	feeble
O' Macaronies shew their Face,	
And think they're free frae Skaith or Harm,	injury
While Pith befriends their Leaders Arm:	strength
Yet fearfu' aften o' their Maught,	might
They quatt the Glory o' the Faught	quit; fight
To this same Warrior wha led	
Thae Heroes to bright Honour's Bed . . .	these

In these lines Fergusson portrays the "Bruiser" from a satiric point of view, emphasizing the coarseness of the man, his crude, primitive instincts, and blind brutality. The picture of his being egged on to "Glory" by the "feckless Race" of cowardly toadies is disgusting enough in itself. But Fergusson does not allow this feeling of disgust at the bruiser to develop in his reader's mind. He immediately modifies it in the very next couplet, and places the bruiser's behavior in another light:

And aft the hack o' Honour shines	often; scar
In Bruiser's Face wi' broken Lines . . .	

With this brilliant and sensitive stroke, Fergusson, in a single couplet, controls his reader's reaction to the whole scene, and reveals his own attitude toward and judgment of the conduct of both bruiser and macaronies. The point that Fergusson is making is that the behavior of the bruiser is far from admirable but that of the macaronies who have goaded him on is a great deal worse. The bruiser is an ignorant and barbarous creature, but at least he has courage and a certain sense of honor; he is not contemptible. The macaronies, on the other hand, who take advantage of the bruiser and leave him in the lurch, have neither courage nor honor and are wholly despicable. Fergusson exposes this "feckless Race" as parasites and frauds, but at the same time he elicits sympathy for the bruiser. This passage is remarkable both for the moral judgment it implies and for the brilliant way in which Fergusson modifies and changes our original impression of the bruiser by contrasting his conduct with that of the macaronies.

In his next verse paragraph Fergusson portrays the macaroni in another situation. For relentless realism and sharp satiric power these lines are unsurpassed in Fergusson:

WHAN Feet in dirty Gutters plash,	splash
And Fock to wale their Fitstaps fash;	choose; footsteps take care
At night the Macaroni drunk,	
In Pools or Gutters aftimes sunk:	
Hegh! what a Fright he now appears,	
When he his Corpse dejected rears!	
Look at that Head, and think if there	
The Pomet slaister'd up his Hair!	pomatum plastered
The Cheeks observe, where now cou'd shine	
The scancing Glories o' Carmine?	shining

Ah, Legs! in vain the Silk-worm there
Display'd to View her eidant Care; busy
For Stink, instead of Perfumes, grow,
And clarty Odours fragrant flow. filthy

As John Speirs very acutely observes of this passage, "the richness of this magnificent comic poetry arises from its unusual combinations of images and sharp contrasts." [14] The "Corpse" and "Gutter" associations contrast with the idea of pomatum and rouge, suggestive of elegance and finery; and these contrasts culminate, as Speirs points out, in the last two couplets, in the superbly restrained and suggestive "Ah, Legs!" image, and in the final juxtaposition of "Stink" and "Perfumes," "clarty" and "fragrant." Through his skillful use of these contrasts, Fergusson succeeds, without explicitly describing the scene, in rendering an astonishingly precise and powerful impression of its filth and loathsomeness as seen from a satiric and semi-humorous point of view. Perhaps the most striiking thing about the passage is its admirable restraint. At least half of the power and vividness of this description lies in what Fergusson does *not* tell the reader. He merely suggests certain aspects of the scene in such a way that the reader's imagination is stirred and induced to fill in the rest of the details.

The principle of contrast operates in "Auld Reikie" on two levels: in the imagery of individual passages, as in the lines just cited, where it is an inherent characteristic of the style; and, on a larger scale, in the overall arrangement of the poem. The way in which this principle of contrast works out on the structural level may be illustrated from Fergusson's arrangement of his night scenes in this major section of the poem and of the morning scenes which follow. In his verse paragraphs on the bruiser and on the drunken macaroni rising from the gutter, Fergusson is treating the more sordid and disgusting aspects of Edinburgh night life. In his next passage, however, when he begins to tell of the clubs and societies, the mood suddenly changes as Fergusson starts to develop another side of the picture. Here the emphasis is on a more wholesome conviviality:

Now mony a Club, jocose and free,
Gie a' to Merriment and Glee . . . give all

The genial, light-hearted mood of these passages abruptly

changes, however, at the end of the lines on the Cape Club where Fergusson suddenly pauses to describe in gruesome detail a passing funeral. These lines, with their references to a "painted Corp" and the "Dead-deal" (a board for laying out corpses), and their excessive emphasis on the frightfulness of death, smack of morbidity and are suggestive of that neurotic streak in Fergusson which caused him to feel an unnatural terror at the thought of sickness and death and which undoubtedly contributed to his final collapse.

Yet this ghastly funeral scene is immediately followed by a charming description of the vegetable market which was in those days held in the High Street between St. Giles and the Tron-Kirk. He then touches on the bits of pastoral freshness, the trees and flower-pots, which brighten even the grimy old city and "Ca' [drive] far awa' the Morning Smell." Next comes an extraordinary lyrical outburst apostrophizing "Nature," including the natural beauties of a girl:

O Nature! canty, blyth and free,	happy
Whare is there Keeking-glass like thee?	looking-glass
Is there on Earth that can compare	
Wi' Mary's Shape, and Mary's Air,	
Save the empurpl'd Speck, that grows	
In the saft Faulds of yonder Rose?	soft folds

The lyric tone and emotional quality of these lines are unusual in Fergusson and are strongly suggestive of the lyrical style of Burns. They are followed, significantly, by a passage on the filth and nauseating smells of the Edinburgh "flesh-market."

The summary given above of two major sections of the poem should be enough to show how basic is the method of dramatic contrast in "Auld Reikie." Fergusson is attempting to catch the essential spirit of the old city and to fix it forever in terms of its strangely contrasting moods. He shows the sordidness and bestiality of Edinburgh night life side by side with its friendliness, its genial goodfellowship and spirited conviviality; he contrasts the greenery of the vegetable stalls in the High Street and the sweet freshness of trees and flowers with the foul stink and filth of the "flesh-market." The constant shifting of scene and mood and the bold juxtaposition of ugliness and beauty give the poem a high degree of realism and dramatic force. The imagination of the reader is excited by the sharpness and suggestiveness of the poem's details, as one sharply-etched portrait after another flashes before his eyes and the whole bustling, colorful panorama of eighteenth-century Edinburgh gradually takes shape.

Two or three passages of the latter part of the poem demand special comment. Fergusson's attack on Sunday hypocrisy is one of the most biting satiric passages in the poem. It reads, in part, as follows:

ON Sunday here, an alter'd Scene	
O' Men and Manners meets our Ein:	eyes
Ane wad maist trow some People chose	almost
To change their Faces wi' their Clo'es,	
And fain wad gar ilk Neighbour think	make each
They thirst for Goodness, as for Drink:	
But there's an unco Dearth o' Grace,	strange
That has nae Mansion but the Face,	
And never can obtain a Part	
In benmost Corner of the Heart.	innermost

Fergusson here uses a more direct method of attack than is usual with him. The undeniable effectiveness of the passage lies chiefly in its sharply satiric phrasing, skillful use of rime, and, above all, in its imaginative force, especially in the brilliant simile, "They thirst for Goodness, as for Drink." The same kind of direct, keen-edged satire is evident again a few lines later in the poem in which Fergusson derides the pretentious Sunday strollers in a passage which is reminiscent of the stanzas on the "barber spark" in "Braid Claith":

WHILE dandring Cits delight to stray	strolling citizens
To Castlehill, or Public Way,	
Whare they nae other Purpose mean,	
Than that Fool Cause o' being seen . . .	

The terse, biting, epigrammatic quality of these touches of direct satire in "Auld Reikie" reminds us of the polished couplets of the great English neo-Classical satirists, especially of Pope, Swift, and Gay, to whom Fergusson is unquestionably indebted in a general way.

The poem ends fittingly on a note of inimitable wit in a short verse paragraph which is worth quoting in full:

REIKIE, farewell! I ne'er cou'd part
Wi' thee but wi' a dowy heart; sad
Aft frae the *Fifan* coast I've seen, often
Thee tow'ring on thy summit green;
So glowr the saints when first is given stare
A fav'rite keek o' glore and heaven; peek; glory
On earth nae mair they bend their ein, eyes
But quick assume angelic mein;
So I on *Fife* wad glowr no more,
But gallop'd to EDINA's shore. Edinburgh's

The humorous force of this farewell is irresistible. Fergusson's profound affection for the old grey city is given comical, half satiric expression through his use of a mock-epic simile. In its irrepressible waggery and imaginative daring the passage seems to epitomize Fergusson's whole poetic personality. The scintillating wit of the passage, its richness in humorous suggestiveness, arise from the comic irony of Fergusson's comparison of Edinburgh and heaven in the light of what has gone before and from the impish tone of his phrasing in such superb lines as "A fav'rite keek of glore and heaven." The ironical force of the comparison, it may be noted, is underlined by his happy choice of the adjective "angelic." Yet, in spite of the conscious irony of his praise of Auld Reekie, Fergusson manages to convey in these lines the impression that he sincerely loves this strangely beautiful, historic, battered, incredibly crowded, and squalid old city of his birth.

"Auld Reikie" is an extraordinarily attractive and powerful poem and, as Fergusson's last major work, forms a fitting climax to his poetic career. It ranks as one of his four or five very best poems, and it is certainly the most comprehensive and impressive of Fergusson's many treatments of eighteenth-century Edinburgh life. Had he been given the time and encouragement to complete his original design of the poem, it would probably have developed to epic proportions; and, judging by the quality of what he actually did write, it might well have become one of the major classics of eighteenth-century poetry. As it stands, the poem is a little classic, and is undoubtedly one of the finest poetic treatments of city life in British literature. In the work of no other Scottish poet is there anything comparable to it.

Sometime during January of 1774, just a few weeks after he

finished work on his last vernacular poems, Fergusson collapsed; and nine months later he was dead. It should be obvious to the most casual reader of Fergusson's poems that until the very eve of his collapse the power and range of his creative imagination were steadily increasing. During the last five months of his active career he produced much of his most brilliant and original work, including "To the Principal and Professors," "The Election," "Elegy on Hogg," "A Drink Eclogue," "To My Auld Breeks," and "Auld Reikie." There is no hint of exhaustion or decline in these poems; rather, they show Fergusson broadening his scope and developing greater artistic control and maturity, experimenting with new subjects and forms, and increasing his mastery of his favorite genres.

CHAPTER 6

Fergusson and Burns: Conclusion

WITH "Auld Reikie"—Fergusson's final and climactic masterpiece of comprehensive realism—his significant poetical career came to an end. It is worthwhile at this point to look back over the Scots poems of 1772-73 and to summarize as concisely as possible the distinguishing features of Fergusson's work and to come to some general conclusions as to the true nature of his achievement from both the historical and purely literary points of view.

I *Fergusson's Qualities as a Poet*

The historical importance of Fergusson's work is two-fold: it lies both in his innovation and development of forms and genres and in the intrinsic quality of his performance within these forms and genres. The changes and innovations he made in particular Scots poetic forms not only represent an original contribution to the growth of the tradition in general, but are of more specific interest for their profound effect upon the work of Burns. In the first place, Fergusson was the first Scottish poet to exploit the full potentialities of the "Habbie" stanza, a form which had come to be used exclusively for the comic elegy and the rimed epistle. Perceiving the possibilities of this stanza, Fergusson broke through the narrow limitations and stereotyped formulas of the "Habbie" tradition, and applied the stanza to several new purposes and kinds of subject matter. In "The Daft-Days," "The King's Birth-Day," "Caller Oysters," "Caller Water," and other pieces, he developed an original type of Scottish poem: the poem of humorous social description in the six-line stanza.

In "Braid Claith" he used the same meter for pure satire, while in the "Elegy on Scots Music" he adapted the "Habbie" stanza as a vehicle for serious rather than comic poetry. Finally, in "To the Tron-Kirk Bell" he revived the ancient "flyting" tradition and used the Habbie stanza for the first time in Scottish poetry for a "flyting" poem. In all of these ways Fergusson's development and extension of the "Habbie" tradition led directly to Burns's even more versatile use of the form.

Fergusson brought about almost equally important developments in other genres, especially in the "Christis Kirk" tradition and in Scottish pastoralism. In "Hallow-fair" and "Leith Races" he introduced a modification of the traditional stanza, a modification which was to be adopted by Burns in "The Holy Fair" and in "Hallowe'en." In "The Election" he extended the subject matter of the genre to include political as well as social satire, and in so doing gave Burns the hint for his further development of the "Christis Kirk" form as a vehicle for clerical satire. In the realm of Scottish pastoralism, Fergusson departed even more radically from eighteenth-century tradition. Though his first effort in this genre, the "Eclogue on Wilkie," is conventional enough (being closely modeled on the pastoral eclogues of Ramsay), in "An Eclogue" Fergusson went far beyond Ramsay in the direction of realism and developed a new type of Scottish pastoralism, treating country life from a humorous point of view, with intimate, homely details and convincing character types, yet remaining within the conventional form of the pastoral eclogue. In "The Farmer's Ingle" he portrayed Scottish farm life with the same kind of unpretentious realism, but with a serious rather than a comic emphasis, while his daring and successful experiment with Spenserian stanzas determined Burns's choice of the same form for his "Cotter's Saturday Night." Fergusson demonstrated in these two poems that interesting and meaningful poetry could be made out of the most ordinary and homely details of rural life, and Burns was quick to take the hint.

Several other innovations which Fergusson introduced may be listed briefly. In "Plainstanes and Causey" and in "A Drink Eclogue" he created an entirely new poetic form, the "flyting eclogue," by combining the old Scottish "flyting" genre with the pastoral eclogue form; and, in so doing, he provided Burns with the models for his "Brigs of Ayr." Furthermore, in several of his poems Fergusson treated themes of satire which had been virtually untouched by earlier eighteenth-century poets in Scotland. He introduced legal satire in "Plainstanes and Causey," the "Rising" and "Sitting of the Session," and other poems, and a sharp element of political satire in "The Ghaists" and "The Election." In "Auld Reikie," moreover, there is a very suggestive passage of religious satire, a theme which Ramsay had already touched upon in his "Elegy on John Cowper," and which Burns was to develop brilliantly. The theme of Scottish patriotism, also touched upon by Ramsay, was given far more conspicuous emphasis by Fergusson in such poems as "Elegy on Scots Music," "The Ghaists," "To the Principal and Professors," "Hame Content," and "A Drink Eclogue"; and so it passed on to Burns. Finally, Fergusson was chiefly responsible for domesticating the English meditative nature poem in Scottish eighteenth-century verse. He attempted this genre with increasing success in the odes to the "Bee," "Butterfly," and "Gowdspink"; and he supplied Burns with Scottish precedent for his "To a Mouse," "To a Mountain Daisy," and other works of this type.

In one respect Fergusson stands alone among Scottish poets: no other comes near him in his brilliant poetic treatment of city life. It was, of course, perfectly natural and appropriate that he should find the materials for his poetry in the life of the Edinburgh he loved and knew intimately, just as it was natural for Burns to write about the rural community in which he lived. But Fergusson's Edinburgh poems form a class by themselves; there is nothing comparable to them in Scottish poetry; and, indeed, in their scope, their vividness, their penetrative, many-sided vision, they must rank among the finest poetic treatments of city life in all British literature. What Fergusson did for Edinburgh life, Burns was presently to do for Scottish farm life; and Burns was to follow Fergusson's lead in building his poetry out of the stuff of everyday experience.

In all of these ways, then, Fergusson was breaking new ground, making his individual contributions to the growth of the great vernacular tradition of which he is a part, and preparing the way for Burns. But Fergusson did more than this: he wrote poems which are important, not merely because they broke with the tradition or modified the tradition in the several ways noted above, but also because they are permanently valuable in themselves as works of art. Fergusson's work has never received adequate recognition for its own sake. Most historians of literature and commentators on Fergusson tend to neglect the intrinsic quality of his work, or to brush over it with brief, uncritical appraisals; they speak as though Fergusson's poems had no life and being of their own—as though they existed only because of Burns. Yet, as I have tried to demonstrate in previous chapters, Fergusson's vernacular poetry, aside from its historical significance or its influence on Burns, is vitally interesting, often powerful, and eminently readable for its own sake. It has, moreover, a unique and highly personalized flavor which sets it apart from the work of any other Scottish poet.

Several characteristics of Fergusson's work distinguish it from that of Hamilton of Gilbertfield, Ramsay, Ross, and other eighteenth-century predecessors. In the first place, there is his bold poetic imagination, essentially a comic imagination, revealing itself both in his daringly original conceptions of entire poems and in his shrewd, penetrating grasp of significant detail. Such poems as the sharp-edged and powerful "Braid Claith"; the delightful fantasies, "Plainstanes and Causey" and "To My Auld Breeks"; and such brilliant comic extravaganzas as "Hallow-fair," "Leith Races," "The Election," and "Auld Reikie"—all these show that he possessed creative powers of a high order. Fergusson's imagination, though narrower in its range than Ramsay's, is infinitely finer in quality, more daring and, at the same time, more sensitive and perceptive. His humor has greater depth and richness than Ramsay's, and certainly more delicacy. His view of life is predominantly comic: he has the rare faculty of finding humor everywhere in the life around him, and, what is even rarer, the ability to select, organize, and communicate his experience through poetic art. He far surpasses Ramsay in his unerring choice of significant details, in his keen eye for humorous incongruities, and, consequently, in his ability to make the most unpromising materials richly suggestive and meaningful.

Fergusson's poetry is, furthermore, remarkable for its pictorial qualities and for its sane and comprehensive realism. Many of his poems are series of vivid little pictures, each illustrating a different aspect of the whole subject and contributing to the total effect. Particularly deft at using dramatic contrast as a satiric method, he shows in poem after poem a surprisingly mature insight into human motives and behavior and an unfailing skill at revealing human incongruities. Fergusson's satire, moreover, is generally good-natured and tolerant in tone, except when he is dealing with sham or meanness of soul. His reaction to a situation is usually two-fold, both intellectual and emotional, the one modifying the other; his keen-eyed satiric vision is often balanced by a degree of sympathy with the human failings of others or by his recognition of compensatory good qualities. This broadminded attitude in Fergusson, his clear-sighted, yet comprehensive, balanced realism, is one of the most fundamental and attractive features of his work.

Fergusson's style is an inseparable part of his poetic imagination and personality. When we consider the tragic brevity of Fergusson's career, the high degree of technical skill and the distinctive personal style which he managed to develop are equally astonishing. His craftsmanship is generally precise and finished, yet he does not allow his disciplined attention to form and technique to inhibit the vitality of his expression. His mastery of particular verse forms, as we have seen, increased rapidly and steadily during his two most prolific years, until he was producing toward the end almost consistently brilliant poems, little masterpieces of conscious, skilled artistry. Fergusson's technical superiority to Ramsay shows most clearly in such poems as "The King's Birth-Day," "Braid Claith," "Hallow-fair," "Leith Races," "The Election," and "To My Auld Breeks," in which he succeeds in reproducing the natural, vigorous rhythms of actual speech, while remaining within the rigid limitations of the verse form. Fergusson handles difficult and exacting stanza forms with ease and fluency, especially in the later poems. For vigor combined with perfection of form, many passages in Fergusson are unsurpassed in Scottish poetry, even by Burns. Burns's work was, in fact, greatly benefited by the examples of technical brilliance set by Fergusson.

The personal flavor of Fergusson's style is more difficult to define than its technical virtues. Though he seldom brings himself directly into his writings, Fergusson's poetry communicates a sense of his buoyant and attractive personality, characterized by audacity, irreverence, impish waggery, geniality, shrewdness, tolerance, sensitivity, keen observation, dry penetrating wit, and abounding vitality. He has a wonderfully rich and suggestive command of Edinburgh vernacular, the "brave metropolitan utterance," as Stevenson called it; and he exploits the subtle possibilities of that language as Ramsay never did. In his command of his own vigorous mother tongue, Fergusson shows the imaginative instinct of the true poet. He has a fine feeling for words, an unerring sense of the right word, for the precise, expressive idiom. The sharpness and conciseness of his imagery, its rich suggestiveness, may be easily illustrated from any of his better poems. Take, for example, these lines from "Hallow-fair"—

> Upo' the tap o' ilka lum
> The sun began to keek . . .

or these from "To My Auld Breeks"—

> As mony a time
> Wi' you I've speel'd the braes o' rime . . .

or from "To the Principal and Professors"—

> Mair hardy, souple, steive an' swank,
> Than ever stood on SAMY's shank.

Fergusson's style, as may be seen from the last lines cited above, has not only muscular vitality and precision, but a peculiar kind of "pawkiness," a quietly humorous flavor. He has a way of giving droll and original expression to almost any idea. This "pawkiness" is an integral part of Fergusson's style and of his distinctive, lovable poetic personality.

Something should be said, finally, about Fergusson's precocious grasp of characterization. As we have seen, he became adept at revealing character briefly and vividly, both through direct description and through dialogue. He shows, in such portraits as those of the barber in "Braid Claith," Robin Gibb in "The Rising of the Session," the cobbler in "The Election," and the "bruiser" in "Auld Reikie," an almost Chaucerian ability to suggest the whole character of the man in a few bold strokes through highlighting significant details. He manages in a few trenchant lines to reveal the essence of characters and scenes in a flash, without stooping to caricature. Perhaps his greatest successes in characterization, however, are achieved through dialogue in which the poet, instead of describing the character, makes the character reveal himself. The speakers in Fergusson's brilliant duologues—Sandie and Willie, Plainstanes and Causey, Brandy and Whisky—are all made real and convincing by this method. Plainstanes, in particular, is a triumph of humorous and dramatic characterization. Similarly, the speeches of Sawny and Jock Bell in "Hallow-fair," of the captain in "Leith Races," and of "John" and "cooper Will" in "The Election" are superbly effective in giving concrete, precise, and vivid impressions of the several speakers. Fergusson's mastery of poetic dialogue is, in fact, unsurpassed in eighteenth-century Scottish verse for vigor, naturalness, and power of suggestion. The depth of understanding Fergusson shows in his delineation of character, his clear-sighted perception of the essential elements and motives in human behavior, are extraordinary in so young a poet.

II *Influence on Burns*

The intrinsic excellence of Fergusson's best work has historical importance as well as purely esthetic value. His poems appeared just in time to save the vernacular revival from dying out altogether. Their sprightliness, craftsmanship, and broad popular appeal served to refresh the lagging vernacular tradition in poetry and to give renewed impetus to the whole movement. Fergusson's sudden emergence, moreover, helped to reassemble and restimulate a popular reading public for Scots verse, without which the tremendous success of Burns would have been impossible. But the intrinsic brilliance of Fergusson's poems did more than this: it provided Burns with examples of high quality in vernacular poetry such as he could never have found in the works of Ramsay. Fergusson's careful workmanship, his mastery of language, and, above all, the boldness and brilliance of his poetic imagination opened Burns's eyes to the full possibilities of the vernacular as a poetic medium.

Fergusson showed Burns that he need not go far afield for the subject matters and language of his poetry, that the light of imagination could be thrown over the humblest objects of the life around him; and, above all, he demonstrated to him, as Ramsay never could, how to make finely wrought, interesting, and meaningful poetry out of such homely subjects from everyday life as "braid claith," "caller oysters," and "auld breeks." Ramsay, too, had treated common life vigorously in some of his works, but he lacked the bold imagination and the artistry necessary to give such subjects permanent value as works of art. Within the relatively narrow range of his best work, Fergusson gave Burns examples of high quality, power, and precision in vernacular poetry; and Burns never forgot the lesson or underestimated its value to him in his own creative practice.[1]

We know from Burns's autobiographical letter to Dr. Moore and from a notation in his *First Commonplace Book* that he "discovered" Fergusson's poems for the first time about August, 1784. As Frank Beaumont has pointed out,[2] the contrast between Burns's poems written before and after his reading of Fergusson attests to the impact of Fergusson's poems upon Burns's creative imagination. The experimental poems of the Mount Oliphant period (1766-1777) are mostly feeble imitations of the genteel English poets—Pope, Addison, Shenstone, Gray, and others—and of Shakespeare. During Burns's residence at Lochlea farm, though he was still very much under the spell of Shenstone's "Elegies," his powers began to mature steadily, as evidenced by such promising pieces as "The Death and Dying Words of Puir Mailie," and two good songs, "Mary Morison" and "The Rigs o' Barley." Despite these promising indications, the bulk of Burns's work during these early years is definitely inferior and imitative.

Then, in late 1784, he discovered Fergusson; and a new and vital development of Burns's genius was almost immediately apparent. Shenstone, the "divine Shenstone," his former bosom favorite, was eclipsed and forgotten; for Burns, stimulated by the brilliance and suggestiveness of Fergusson's poems, turned his energies toward the native poetic tradition where his real strength lay, and began to pour out, with breathtaking speed and fecundity, that magnificent series of vernacular masterpieces written in 1785 and 1786, beginning with the "Epistle to Davie"; "Holy Willie's Prayer"; "Death and Doctor Hornbook"; the epistles to Lapraik, Simson, Goldie, and M'Math; "Hallowe'en"; "To a Mouse"; "The Jolly Beggars"; "Address to the Deil"; and so on to "The Twa Dogs", "The Holy Fair," and many others. Fergusson was unquestionably the primary literary force behind Burns's upsurge of creative activity during these, his greatest and most fruitful years.

In poem after poem Fergusson's influence can be seen operating on Burns's imagination, suggesting themes, ideas, verse forms, satiric devices, descriptive methods, expressive words and phrases which stuck in Burns's subconscious memory. So profound and interpenetrative was this influence that we must conclude that Burns read and reread his Fergusson, virtually memorizing the poems until they became a part of his own thought and feeling. In almost every major poem that Burns wrote during these two wonderful years, traces of Fergusson can be discerned—stimulating, suggesting, and, to some extent, directing Burns's creative activity.

The many different ways in which Fergusson's poems operated on Burns's imagination have already been touched on and need only be summarized briefly. In the years before he met with Fergusson's work, Burns had used the "Habbie" stanza very seldom, in some three or four poems. Fergusson's brilliant handling of the form, however, seems to have opened Burns's eyes to its possibilities since, shortly after his reading of Fergusson, he began to use it with increasing frequency in poem after poem. Similarly, Fergusson's work in the "Christis Kirk" stanza prompted Burns to try his hand at the form; and it is significant that in his first attempt, "Hallowe'en," Burns used Fergusson's special form of the stanza. Other Scottish poetic forms used by Fergusson in his own original way were soon taken over by Burns, including the rimed epistle, the duologue form ("The Twa Dogs" and "Brigs of Ayr"), the serious description of farm life in Spenserian stanzas ("The Cotter's Saturday Night"), the meditative nature poem ("To a Mouse"), and Fergusson's original "flyting eclogue" ("Brigs of Ayr"). Besides taking over these poetic forms and genres developed by the Edinburgh poet, Burns modeled several poems directly and, no doubt, consciously on Fergusson: "The Cotter's Saturday Night" on "The Farmer's Ingle," "Scotch Drink" on "Caller Water" and "A Drink Eclogue," "The Holy Fair" on "Leith Races" and "Hallow-fair," "Brigs of Ayr" on "Plainstanes and Causey," and so forth.

But Fergusson's influence was far more diffuse and interpenetrative than these obvious manifestations would indicate. We find Burns taking up again and again themes and methods of satire which he found in Fergusson, and re-working them in the light of his own experience. Traces of Fergusson's style; of Fergusson's quietly humorous tone; of Fergusson's distinctive kind of insinuative, "pawky," satiric humor; of his actual phraseology

—all of these crop up in poem after poem of Burns, often in poems which are generally unlike anything that Fergusson ever wrote. Sometimes too, Burns made use of suggestions from Fergusson's worthless English poems, a fact which proves how thoroughly saturated his mind was with all of Fergusson's works, good and bad.

On the whole, however, Fergusson's example was of incalculable value to Burns; no other poet had so decisive an effect upon his work. Fergusson seems to be ever-present in Burns himself, his influence operating just beneath the surface of Burns's conscious mind, acting as a kind of poetic catalyst, prompting and stimulating Burns to creative activity. Burns, in fact, found himself in Fergusson; he saw in Fergusson's unfulfilled career the key to his own poetic ambitions and desires, and he set to work with a will to continue and complete what Fergusson had so brilliantly begun.

In comparing the poetry of Fergusson and Burns, one must recognize the greater range and maturity of Burns's imagination. There is no hint in Fergusson, for example, of the spontaneous and powerful lyric impulse which made Burns one of the great song writers of all time, nor of Burns's deep feeling of kinship with nature so movingly expressed in such poems as "To a Mouse." Moreover, for all Fergusson's imaginative audacity, he shows little of Burns's social and political radicalism, of the sweep and passion of Burns's art. Burns's essentially passionate nature, bursting the bonds of restraint that the Kirk would have imposed upon him, leads him to attack the Kirk itself and to a freer and franker expression in a greater variety of matters than Fergusson would have dared to undertake. Burns dares to go to the roots of his own being and to speak his heart out in his poetry. He feels compelled to do so. There is none of this intense subjectivity in Fergusson; rather, he tends to be reticent about himself in his writing.

Fergusson is, in fact, essentially conservative in his attitudes. He was living in times which, notwithstanding the unrest in Scotland resulting from the Union of 1707 and the Jacobite rebellion of 1745, were generally stable, politically and socially. Though Fergusson is quick to satirize the abuses and shortcomings he perceives in the society of his day, he never goes so far as to attack the social structure itself. The American and

French revolutions, however, coming a few years after Fergusson's death, and accompanied by a general upheaval of European society, acted as direct and potent stimuli upon the imagination of Burns; and they partially account for the radical, and defiantly democratic elements in his poetry. Burns's naturally rebellious nature and the fact that he was a peasant rather than a graduate of St. Andrews also had much to do with the intensity of his political views. Fergusson lived in less exciting years, but he seems also to have possessed a kind of genial tolerance, a willingness to accept the world as he found it, without feeling compelled to change it. Thus the vivid little world of his art is generally undisturbed by current philosophical questions. Fergusson excels at humorous social description, and within this relatively narrow range the vitality and artistry of his work has seldom been surpassed in Scots poetry, even by Burns.

III *Final Evaluation*

In coming to a final evaluation of Fergusson's achievement, we must never forget his youthfulness, the extreme brevity of his career, and the crushing difficulties under which he worked. All of his best poetry was produced during a period of twenty-four months, and his poetical career was ended when he was twenty-three. Burns during the first twenty-three years of his life produced nothing comparable to Fergusson's achievement. Fergusson, then, like his English contemporary Chatterton, is one of the unfulfilled possibilities of our literature. Up to the moment of his collapse, as we have seen, Fergusson was increasing in stature and maturity as a creative artist. Had he lived, there is little doubt that he would have seriously rivaled Burns, at least as a satirist and as a writer of humorous descriptive poetry, if not as a lyricist. Additionally, it may safely be said that, had it not been for Fergusson's achievement, Burns would not have been the Burns that we know as the great national poet of Scotland. Part of Burns's glory belongs, in a very real sense, to Robert Fergusson.

But judged on merit alone, Fergusson's poetry deserves higher rank and recognition than it has hitherto received. Though small in bulk and relatively narrow in scope, his work is unquestionably the finest body of poetry produced in Scotland during the eighteenth century before Burns. Fergusson deserves a permanent place among the classics of Scottish poetry, ranking not too far below Dunbar and Burns. In the wider field of British literature, he remains necessarily a minor poet—but a minor poet of extraordinary quality and interest. He breaks new ground in poetry, not by breaking with the established poetic traditions, but by putting the traditions to new uses. As the English Romantic poets a generation later were to exploit such older forms as the Spenserian stanza, blank verse, and the heroic couplet, so Fergusson revitalized the traditional forms of Scottish verse.

Aside from a place in literary history, Fergusson's work has a perennial freshness and enduring appeal. He makes old Edinburgh live again as no other writer has ever done. Fergusson's objective realism; the sharpness, vividness, and finished artistry of his style; the genial, insinuative tone of his humor; and the bold, yet sensitive and highly personal quality of his imagination combine to make his poetry especially attractive to modern tastes. It is to be hoped that in the years to come his reputation will increase, that there will be a rediscovery, a new and more genuine appreciation of Fergusson as one of the little masters.

Notes and References

Chapter One

1. *The Letters of Robert Burns,* ed. J. De Lancey Ferguson (Oxford, 1931), I, 72. Burns obtained permission from the authorities and, at his own expense, raised a handsome stone over Fergusson's grave which remains to this day the only important memorial to Fergusson in Edinburgh.

2. "Apostrophe to Fergusson" in *The Poetry of Robert Burns,* eds. Wm. E. Henley and Thos. F. Henderson, Centenary Ed. (Edinburgh, 1896-97), II, 211.

3. Alexander Peterkin in his edition of *The Works of Robert Fergusson* (London, 1807), p. 53, states, on the testimony of an unnamed informant who had known Fergusson, that the poet's ailment was syphilis. Fergusson's most recent biographer, Matthew P. McDiarmid, in his *The Poems of Robert Fergusson,* Scottish Text Soc., 3rd Ser. 21 (Edinburgh, 1954), I, 68-70, accepts this explanation; but the evidence is slender indeed.

4. About this date, see McDiarmid (note 3 above), I, 77-78.

Chapter Two

1. Alexander B. Grosart in *Robert Fergusson* (Edinburgh, 1898), p. 53, claims to have found Fergusson's draft of this ode among the Ruddiman MSS., "in a very boyish hand, as though it had been a High School exercise." The deftness of the translation, however, makes this extremely early dating hard to believe, since Fergusson was a mere child of twelve when he left the High School of Edinburgh in 1762.

2. See Hamilton's *Poems on Several Occasions* (Glasgow, 1749), p. 116. The works of Ramsay, Fergusson, and Burns are so easily available in a wide variety of editions that it seems useless, in citing their poems, to give volume and page references to particular editions. In this study, all quotations from Ramsay and Burns are taken from *The Works of Allan Ramsay,* eds. Burns Martin and John W. Oliver, Scottish Text Soc., 3rd Ser. 19, 20 (Edinburgh, 1953); and *The Poetry of Robert Burns,* eds. Wm. E. Henley and Thos. F. Henderson,

Centenary Ed. (Edinburgh, 1896-97). For quotations of Fergusson's poems, I have used the following texts: (1) *Poems* (Edinburgh, 1773), the first collected edition, for all poems therein, most of which were reprinted from *The Weekly Magazine* under Fergusson's personal supervision with some minor corrections; (2) *The Weekly Magazine* for all poems which appeared in it, except for those included in the 1773 volume; and (3) *The Poems of Robert Fergusson*, ed. Matthew P. McDiarmid, Scottish Text Soc., 3rd Ser. 24 (Edinburgh, 1956), for those few poems which appeared neither in the 1773 volume nor in *The Weekly Magazine*.

3. Fergusson could have found the texts of this famous elegy and of its companion piece, the "Elegy on Sanny Briggs," in James Watson's *A Choice Collection of Comic and Serious Scots Poems, both Antient and Modern* (Edinburgh, 1706).

4. Matthew P. McDiarmid, in his fine edition of Fergusson (see note 2 above), asserts (II, 284) that the suggestion for "The Sow of Feeling" came from the Epilogue to Henry Mackenzie's play *The Prince of Tunis* which Fergusson quotes as the motto for his poem. The primary literary source for Fergusson's piece, however, is a passage in the Duke of Buckingham's famous dramatic burlesque *The Rehearsal* (1671) which reads as follows:

> So boar and sow, when any storm is nigh,
> Snuff up, and smell it gath'ring in the sky;
> Boar beckons sow to trot in chestnut groves,
> And there consummate their unfinished loves:
> Pensive, in mud, they wallow all alone,
> And snort and gruntle to each other's moan.
> (I.ii.245-50)

These lines in *The Rehearsal* are themselves a parody of a passage in Dryden's *The Conquest of Granada,* Part II, I.ii. For a discussion of the whole matter, see my article "Robert Fergusson's *The Sow of Feeling* and Buckingham's *The Rehearsal,*" *Notes and Queries,* N. S. IV (Nov., 1957), 485-86.

Chapter Three

1. Noted by Alexander B. Grosart, *Robert Fergusson* (Edinburgh, 1898), p. 140.

2. See David Sillar, *Poems* (Kilmarnock, 1789), p. 61.

3. *The Scottish Tradition in Literature* (Edinburgh and London, 1958), pp. 177-79. Burns was later to use similar patterns of shifting styles for ironic effects; for specific demonstrations of this device in his work, see Allan H. MacLaine, "Burns's Use of Parody in *Tam O'*

Shanter," *Criticism,* I (1959), 308-16; and Richard Morton, "Narrative Irony in Robert Burns's 'Tam o' Shanter'," *Modern Language Quarterly,* XXII (1961), 12-20.

4. This huge cannon, made of iron staves and hoops, was forged in the fifteenth century and saw service in several wars. In 1680 the barrel of Mons Meg burst while firing a salute to the Duke of York (later James II) on his visit to Edinburgh. In 1734 Meg was taken to the Tower of London where she remained until restored by George IV to Edinburgh Castle in 1829.

5. For a full account of the elaborate ceremony of the occasion, see James Logie Robertson, *Furth in Field* (London, 1894), pp. 55 ff.

6. "Eighteenth-Century Vernacular Poetry," in *Scottish Poetry: A Critical Survey,* ed. James Kinsley (London, 1955), p. 176.

7. See *The Poems of John Philips,* ed. M. G. Lloyd Thomas (Oxford, 1927), p. 5.

8. Hamilton's epistles are usually printed in editions of Ramsay together with Ramsay's replies.

9. Compare also Burns's first "Epistle to John Lapraik."

10. For two notes on the probable identification of Fergusson's correspondent with Dr. Andrew Gray, the minister of Abernethy, see Matthew P. McDiarmid, ed., *The Poems of Robert Fergusson,* Scottish Text Soc., 3rd Ser. 21, 24 (Edinburgh, 1954, 1956), I, 43n; II, 290.

11. See, however, Robert Chambers, ed., *The Poetical Works of Robert Fergusson* (Edinburgh, 1840), p. 22, who plausibly suggests that Fergusson may have got the hint for "Braid Claith" from a passage of the Life of Richard Boyse in Colley Cibber's *Lives of the Poets.* The passage is also given in McDiarmid, II, 268.

12. "A Note on Robert Fergusson" in *The Riddle of the Ruthvens* (Edinburgh, 1919), p. 534.

13. *Robert Fergussons Anteil an der Literatur Schottlands* (Heidelberg, 1923), p. 36.

14. *Three Centuries of Scottish Literature* (Glasgow, 1893), II, 42.

15. All of these, except "Peblis" and Skinner's poem, were accessible to Fergusson in Jas. Watson's *Choice Collection* (Edinburgh, 1706-1711), or in Ramsay's *Poems* (Edinburgh, 1721) or his *Ever Green* (Edinburgh, 1724).

16. *Poems,* p. 41. Noted by Grosart in *The Works of Robert Fergusson* (London, 1851), p. 37.

Chapter Four

1. *The Perth Magazine of Knowledge and Pleasure,* published in Perth by Robert Morison. See III, 272-73.

2. *Poems* (Kilmarnock, 1789), p. 38. For closely parallel passages, compare especially Sillar's third stanza with Fergusson's second.

3. This point is made by John Speirs, *The Scots Literary Tradition* (London, 1940), p. 119.

4. This grammatical error was first noticed by Wm. Roughead, *The Riddle of the Ruthvens* (Edinburgh, 1919), p. 535.

5. See, for example, the wrongheaded comments of Frank Beaumont in "Fergusson and Burns: The Shaping of a Poet," *Proceedings of the Royal Philosophical Soc. of Glasgow,* XLII (1911), 87. This generally excellent article is reprinted in *The Annual Burns Chronicle and Club Directory,* O. S. XXII (1913), 83-109.

6. The volumes of 1773 and 1779 are considered together as the first edition of Fergusson. In getting up the 1779 volume, Walter Ruddiman collected from *The Weekly Magazine* and from Fergusson's manuscripts such poems as had not already been printed in the 1773 volume. These poems formed "Part II" of the 1779 edition; the new Part II was bound together with the unsold copies of the 1773 volume ("Part I") and the whole issued in two parts as the first complete edition of Fergusson. Ruddiman's 1782 edition is, therefore, considered as the second and not as the third edition of Fergusson.

7. *The Lives of the Scotish* [sic] *Poets* (Edinburgh, 1804), II, 436.

8. *"For Puir Auld Scotland's Sake"* (Edinburgh, 1887), pp. 115-16.

9. *Robert Burns* (New York, 1950), pp. 150-62.

10. *Scottish Poetry: Drummond of Hawthornden to Fergusson* (Glasgow, 1911), p. 182.

11. *Proc. of Royal Philosophical Soc. of Glasgow,* XLII (1911), 81 ff.

12. Ed. *Works of Robert Fergusson* (London, 1851), p. 66.

13. Like Fergusson's "Ode to the Bee," this poem was omitted from the 1779 edition, and was not reprinted until 1782 when it appeared in Ruddiman's second edition of Fergusson.

14. *Poems on Several Occasions* (Glasgow, 1749), pp. 54-57.

15. *Ibid.,* pp. 135-37.

16. Fergusson's epistle "To Andrew Gray," discussed in the preceding chapter, had appeared in *The Perth Magazine* on July 2.

Chapter Five

1. This line undoubtedly suggested Burns's "A filly buirdly, steeve, an' swank" in stanza 3 of his "Auld Farmer's Salutation."

2. For a detailed account of the procedure for the whole municipal election, see Hugo Arnot, *The History of Edinburgh* (Edinburgh, 1816), pp. 391-94.

3. The last five lines of "A Mauchline Wedding" are clearly modeled

on the second stanza of "The Election." For a full discussion of the relationship, see my article "Some Echoes of Robert Fergusson in Burns's *A Mauchline Wedding,*" *Notes and Queries,* N. S. VIII (July, 1961), 265-66.

4. *The Poetry of Robert Burns* (Edinburgh, 1897), II, 291.

5. "Eighteenth-Century Vernacular Poetry," in *Scottish Poetry: A Critical Survey,* ed. Jas. Kinsley (London, 1955), p. 183.

6. Ed. *Works of Robert Fergusson* (London, 1851), p. 121.

7. John A. Fairley, "A Bibliography of Robert Fergusson," in *Records of the Glasgow Bibliographical Soc.,* III (1914), 128, was the first to give full and accurate data on this poem.

8. *A Choice Collection of Scots Poems, Antient and Modern* (Edinburgh), p. 89.

9. See *The Poems of John Philips,* ed. M. G. Lloyd Thomas (Oxford, 1927), p. 7.

10. This note appears in Burns's Interleaved Copy of the *Museum.* See Wm. E. Henley and Thos. F. Henderson, eds., *The Poetry of Robert Burns,* III, 497. For a discussion of the authorship of the song, see Matthew P. McDiarmid ed. *The Poems of Robert Fergusson,* Scottish Text Soc., 3rd Ser. 24 (Edinburgh, 1956), II, 272-73.

11. McDiarmid (II, 271) sees "no reason to doubt Johnson's attribution."

12. See Irving's *History of Scotish* [sic] *Poetry,* ed. J. A. Carlyle (Edinburgh, 1861), p. 580; and Eyre-Todd ed. *Scottish Poetry of the Seventeenth Century* (Glasgow, 1895), pp. 255, 260.

13. (London), I, 56-59. Fergusson could have found the text of "The Blythsome Bridal" in this same anthology (I, 67-69), or in Jas. Watson's *Choice Collection of Comic and Serious Scots Poems, both Antient and Modern,* in 3 Parts (Edinburgh, 1706, 1709, 1711).

14. *The Scots Literary Tradition* (London, 1940), pp. 120-21.

Chapter Six

1. For exhaustive lists of Burns's specific borrowings from Fergusson, see Max Meyerfeld, *Robert Burns: Studien zu seiner dichterischen Entwicklung* (Berlin, 1899), and Otto Ritter, *Quellenstudien zu Robert Burns,* in *Palaestra,* XX (Berlin, 1901).

2. "Fergusson and Burns," *Proc. of Royal Philosophical Soc. of Glasgow,* XLII (1911), 72-78.

Selected Bibliography

More or less complete bibliographies of Fergusson up to 1955 may be found in John A. Fairley, *A Bibliography of Robert Fergusson* (Glasgow: J. Maclehose and Sons, 1915), supplemented by Matthew P. McDiarmid's edition (1956), II, xv-xxiii, listed below.

PRIMARY SOURCES
COLLECTED EDITIONS OF FERGUSSON

Of over forty separate editions of Fergusson's poems, this list includes only those containing important biographical and critical materials or having special historical interest.

Poems. Edinburgh: Walter and Thos. Ruddiman, 1773.

Poems on Various Subjects. Edinburgh: Walter and Thos. Ruddiman, 1779. In two parts, Part I being unsold copies of the 1773 edition, Part II containing uncollected and posthumous pieces.

Poetical Works of Robert Fergusson. With life by David Irving. Glasgow: Chapman and Lang, 1800.

The Works of Robert Fergusson. With life [by Alexander Peterkin]. London: S. A. and H. Oddy, 1807.

The Poems of Robert Fergusson. With life and criticism by James Bannington. London: A. Macpherson, 1809.

The Poems of Robert Fergusson. With life and criticism by James Gray. Edinburgh: John Fairbairn, etc., 1821.

The Poetical Works of Robert Fergusson. With life and notes by Robert Chambers. Edinburgh: Wm. and Robt. Chambers, 1840.

The Works of Robert Fergusson. Ed. with life and criticism by A.B.G. (Alexander Balloch Grosart). London, Edinburgh, and Dublin: A. Fullarton and Co., 1851. This is the first scholarly edition and biography, though marred by many errors.

The Poems of Robert Fergusson. With life by Robert Aiken. Edinburgh: W. J. Hay, 1895.

Poetical Works of Robert Fergusson. With life and notes by Robert Ford. Paisley: A. Gardner, 1905. Inaccuracies in text.

The Scots Poems of Robert Fergusson. Ed. with life and notes by John Telfer. Edinburgh: Scottish Features, 1948.

The Unpublished Poems of Robert Fergusson. Ed. with notes by William E. Gillis. Edinburgh: M. MacDonald, 1955. Seventeen new poems of little merit.

The Poems of Robert Fergusson. Ed. with life, criticism, and notes by Matthew P. McDiarmid. 2 vols. Scottish Text Soc., 3rd Ser. 21, 24. Edinburgh: Wm. Blackwood and Sons, 1954, 1956. By far the best and most complete edition, superseding all others, with excellent biography and notes.

SECONDARY SOURCES

1. General Studies of Scots Literature

This list is limited to a few especially useful works.

Daiches, David. *Robert Burns.* New York: Rhinehart, 1950. Excellent introductory chapter on the Scots poetic tradition, with considerable attention to Fergusson.

Graham, Henry Grey. *Scottish Men of Letters in the Eighteenth Century.* London: A. and C. Black, 1901. An older work, but still valuable, especially on minor writers.

Henderson, Thomas Finlayson. *Scottish Vernacular Literature.* 3rd ed. Edinburgh: John Grant, 1910. For over half a century this was the standard work; still useful, though largely superseded by Wittig (see below).

Smith, George Gregory. *Scottish Literature.* London: Macmillan, 1919.

Speirs, John. *The Scots Literary Tradition.* London: Chatto and Windus, 1940. Solid, interesting short book.

Kinsley, James, ed. *Scottish Poetry: A Critical Survey.* London: Cassell, 1955. An excellent volume of essays by various hands; see especially "Eighteenth-Century Vernacular Poetry" by David Daiches.

Wittig, Kurt. *The Scottish Tradition in Literature.* Edinburgh and London: Oliver and Boyd, 1958. The most recent and best general book on the subject.

2. Some Biographical and Critical Studies of Fergusson

The best biography and some valuable criticism are to be found in McDiarmid's edition listed above.

Beaumont, Frank. "Fergusson and Burns: The Shaping of a Poet," *Proceedings of the Royal Philosophical Society of Glasgow,* XLII (1911), 71-92. Reprinted in *Annual Burns Chronicle and Club Directory,* O. S. XXII (1913), 83-109. A long and important article, still the fullest treatment of the subject, though occasionally unfair to Fergusson.

Campbell, Alexander. *An Introduction to the History of Poetry in Scotland.* Edinburgh: A. Foulis, 1798. Article on Fergusson (288-300) has value as an early biographical sketch.

Chambers, Robert. *A Biographical Dictionary of Eminent Scotsmen.* 4 vols. Glasgow: Blackie and Son, 1835. Important early article on Fergusson's life, II, 296-311.

Douglas, Sir George. *Scottish Poetry: Drummond of Hawthornden to Fergusson.* Glasgow: J. Maclehose and Sons, 1911. Full chapter on Fergusson.

Gleig, George. *Supplement to the Third Edition of the Encyclopedia Britannica.* Edinburgh: T. Bonar, 1801. Early "life" of Fergusson, I, 646-48.

Green, Frederick Charles. *Robert Fergussons Anteil an der Literatur Schottlands.* Heidelberg: C. Winter, 1923. An interesting critical study in German.

Grosart, Alexander Balloch. *Robert Fergusson.* Famous Scots Series. New York: C. Scribner's Sons, 1898. A revision of the life in Grosart's 1851 edition.

Inverarity, James. "Strictures on Irving's Life of Fergusson," *Scots Magazine,* N. S. VIII (1801), 697-701, 763-67. By a relative of the poet.

Irving, David. *The Life of Robert Fergusson.* Glasgow: Chapman and Lang, 1799. The earliest substantial biography.

MacLaine, Allan H. "Robert Fergusson's *Auld Reikie* and the Poetry of City Life," *Studies in Scottish Literature,* I (1963), 99-110.

Ritter, Otto. *Quellenstudien zu Robert Burns, 1773-1791.* Berlin: Mayer and Müller, 1901. Contains detailed evidence of Fergusson's influence on Burns.

Robertson, James Logie ("Hugh Haliburton"). *"For Puir Auld Scotland's Sake."* Edinburgh and London: W. Paterson, 1887. Contains three essays on Fergusson, pp. 79-121.

Roughead, William. "A Note on Robert Fergusson," in *The Riddle of the Ruthvens* (essays). Edinburgh: W. Green and Son, 1919. A perceptive essay.

Smith, Sydney Goodsir, ed. *Robert Fergusson, 1750-1774: Essays by Various Hands to Commemorate the Bicentenary of his Birth.* Edinburgh: Oliver and Boyd, 1952. An extremely valuable compilation, including an excellent introduction by the editor and the following essays: Hugh MacDiarmid, "Robert Fergusson: Direct Poetry and the Scottish Genius"; Douglas Young, "The Making of a Poet: Some Notes on Fergusson's Educational Backgrounds"; John W. Oliver, "Fergusson and *Ruddiman's Magazine*"; John Speirs, "Tradition and Robert Fergusson"; James B. Caird, "Fergusson and Stevenson"; Albert D. Mackie, "Fergusson's Language: Braid Scots Then and Now"; Alexander Law, "A Note on the Bibliography and 'Lives' of Robert Fergusson"; William Montgomerie, "The Scottish Folk-song Tradition in Ramsay, Fergusson and Burns."

Sommers, Thomas. *The Life of Robert Fergusson, The Scottish Poet.* Edinburgh: C. Stewart, 1803. Important early biography by one who knew the poet.

Index

Act of Union, 98-99
Addison, Joseph, 159
Arnot, Hugo, 168n

Beattie, James, "Minstrel," 90
Beaumont, Frank, 90, 159, 168n
"Birks of Indermay," 39
"Blythsome Bridal, The," 65, 141, 169n
Boswell, James, 116
Boyse, Richard, 167n
Buckingham, George Villiers, Duke of, *The Rehearsal*, 166n
Burns, Robert, attitude toward Fergusson, 21, 32 (in quot.), 74 (in quot.), 139-40; compared with Fergusson, 110, 112, 128, 129, 135, 139-40, 142, 148, 152-63; imitations of English poets, 22, 159; indebtedness to Fergusson, 158-63 (summary), 32, 37, 41, 46, 52, 54, 62, 64-65, 75, 78-79, 87, 90, 97, 104, 107-8, 112, 116, 118-20, 124, 125, 130, 132-33, 136, 139, 143, 152-56; letter on Fergusson's grave, 15; *writings of:* "Address to a Haggis," 116; "Address to the Deil," 75, 159; "Address to the Unco Guid," 143; "Auld Farmer's Salutation," 46, 168n; "The Brigs of Ayr," 78-79, 97, 143, 160; "Cotter's Saturday Night," 35, 90-95, 160; "Death and Doctor Hornbook," 125, 159; "The Death and Dying Words of Puir Mailie," 159; "Elegy on Matthew Henderson," 37; "Epistle to a Young Friend," 143; "Epistle to Davie," 159; "Epistle to J. Lapraik," 159, 167n; "Epistle to Kennedy," 54; *First Commonplace Book*, 159; "Hallowe'en," 65, 153, 159-60; "The Holy Fair," 65, 107, 143, 153, 159-60; "Holy Willie's Prayer," 143, 159; "The Jolly Beggars," 41, 124, 159; "The Lea-Rig," 140; "Mary Morison," 142, 159; "A Mauchline Wedding," 120, 168n, 169n; "The Rigs o' Barley," 159; "Scotch Drink," 41, 75, 133, 160; "Tam O'Shanter," 39, 65, 118-20, 166n, 167n; "Tam Samson's Elegy," 37; "Third Epistle to J. Lapraik," 41; "To a Haggis," 46, 48; "To a Louse," 54; "To a Mountain Daisy," 35-36, 87, 154; "To a Mouse," 36, 154, 159-61; "To William Simpson," 136, 159; "The Twa Dogs," 62, 78, 120, 132, 159-60; "Verses to Collector Mitchell," 125; "A Winter Night," 130

Cap-and-Feather Close, 19
Cape Club of Edinburgh, 20, 140, 147-48
Carlyle, J. A., 169n
Carlyle, Thomas, 55
Chambers, Robert, 167n
Charmer, The, 139
Chatterton, Thomas, 162
"Christis Kirk on the Green," 17, 65-67
Christ's Church at the Tron, 70-72, 148
Cibber, Colley, 167n
City Guard, The, 35-36, 43-44, 66, 69, 102, 107-10
Commissary Office, 20, 74, 116, 137
Court of Session, 83, 85, 129-31

Index

Daiches, David, 90, 128, 167n
Deans, Davie, 126
Douglas, Sir George, 90
Drummond, George, 143
Drummond of Hawthornden, William, 17, 104, 118; "Forth Feasting," 104
Dryden, John, "Absalom and Achitophel," 99; *The Conquest of Granada,* 166n
Dumfries Weekly Magazine, 128
Dunbar, William, 16-17, 70, 163; "The Golden Targe," 16; "Tidings frae the Session," 129

Eliot, T. S., 58
Eyre-Todd, George, 140, 169n

Fairley, John A., 169n
Ferguson, J. De Lancey, 165n
Fergusson, Robert, anti-sentimentalism, 29-30; beginnings as a poet, 20-28; brevity of his career, 20-21, 127, 151, 156, 162; career, summary of, 19-21; "Christis Kirk" tradition, 17, 64-67, 72, 83, 90, 106-7, 111, 119-21, 141, 153, 160; city life, 32-37, 40-49, 64-73, 78-86, 106-11, 119-24, 129-31, 142-51, 154; comic elegy tradition, 25-27, 36, 56, 124; conviviality, 33-35, 48, 68-70, 84-86, 127, 144, 147-48; descriptive technique, 33-34, 40, 48-49, 62-64, 66-70, 91-96, 107-10, 113-14, 120-24, 142-50, 155-56; drinking, 34-35, 40-41, 48-49, 68-70, 74-77, 84-86, 107-110, 122-23, 129, 130, 132-35, 137, 144-47; English poems, 20, 22, 27-31, 135, 161; "flyting eclogue," 78-83, 132-35, 160; "flyting" tradition, 70-72, 78, 132, 153; grave, Burns's letter on, 15; "Habbie" stanza form, 24-27, 32-33, 36-37, 40, 50, 54, 70, 72, 74, 83, 124-31, 152-53, 160; heroic couplets, 97-99, 132-35; humor, 19, 26-27, 29-30, 35, 40-44, 50-51, 54-58, 67-70, 71-72, 75-77, 79-83, 85-86, 101-2, 108-10, 116-19, 120-24, 125-28, 133-34, 135-39, 150, 155, 157, 160, 163; humorous social description, 33-34, 40-45, 56-57, 67-70, 84-86, 100-103, 108-10, 120-24, 142-50, 162; imaginative boldness, 39, 40-42, 45, 67-70, 72-73, 78-83, 101-2, 109-11, 116-19, 124, 132-35, 138-39, 142, 148-50, 155, 158, 161, 163; influence of English poets, 22, 28-29, 86-89, 142, 149; influence on Burns, 32, 37, 41, 46, 52, 54, 62, 64-65, 75, 78-79, 87, 90, 97, 104, 107-8, 112, 116, 118-20, 124, 125, 130, 132-33, 136, 139, 143, 152-56, 158-63; legal satire, 83-85, 129-31, 154; materialism, 98, 103, 123, 127, 130; meditative nature poem, 86-89, 100-103, 113-16, 154, 160; nature, 53, 87-89, 113-16, 128, 148; originality, 32, 36, 39, 40-42, 45, 49, 61-65, 72, 78-83, 89-90, 100, 107, 111-12, 115-16, 119-24, 125, 132, 138-39, 142, 152-54, 163; personal qualities, 52-53, 55, 156; personal satire, 26-27, 85, 116-19, 125-28, 155; poetic development, 53-54, 60, 70, 72-73, 88-89, 95-96, 99, 103, 110, 115-16, 120-24, 125, 127-28, 131, 133, 135, 137-39, 140, 150-51; poetic turning point, 30-31; political satire, 96-100, 119-24, 153; poverty, 19, 84-85, 95, 116, 134-39, 143; realism, 55, 61-64, 73, 88-89, 91-96, 109-10, 112, 120-24, 127-28, 142-50, 152-53, 155, 163; religious satire, 49, 149, 153-54; rural life, 38-39, 61-64, 75, 86-96, 153; satire on medical quacks, 47, 76; Scoto-English style, 22-23, 27-31, 35, 37-39, 44, 59-60, 77, 87-89, 105, 114; Scots music, 32, 35, 37-39; Scots nationalism, 18, 37-39, 95, 98-100, 103-6, 116-19, 132-35, 154; Scots pastoralism, 44, 59-64, 72, 77, 86-89, 91-96, 103-6, 113-16, 140, 153; Scots song, 39, 139-42; senti-

mentalism, 28-30, 59-60; skill in characterization, 61-63, 73, 78-83, 85, 92-94, 96, 108, 120-28, 145-47, 153, 157-58; skill in use of dialogue, 62-63, 68-69, 80-82, 110, 121-24, 132-35, 158; social satire, 54-58, 80-83, 103-10, 119-24, 132-35, 142-50, 153, 155; Spenserian stanza, 89-95, 153, 160; structural method, 33, 37, 40, 46-47, 54-58, 65-67, 73, 86, 91-96, 100-110, 113-14, 118-19, 143-50, 156; subjectivity, 88, 115-16, 135-39, 156, 161; superiority over Burns, 78-79, 90, 154; superiority over Ramsay, 43, 51, 59, 155; tetrameter couplets, 86-89, 100, 103-6, 113-19, 135-39, 142-50; use of local dialects, 68, 110; verse epistle tradition, 50--53, 72, 160; *writings of:* "Against Repining at Fortune," 29; "Answer to Mr. J.S.'s Epistle," 50-52, 54, 88; "Auld Reikie," 124, 139, 142-51, 154-55, 157; "Braid Claith," 54-58, 73, 83, 103, 106, 111-12, 135, 139, 149, 153, 155-57, 167n; "Caller Oysters," 45-49, 73, 139, 152; "Caller Water," 74-78, 111, 152, 160; "The Daft-Days," 20, 22-23, 32-37, 65, 73, 84, 104, 152; "Damon to his Friends, A Ballad," 29; "A Drink Eclogue," 132-35, 151, 153-54, 160; "Dumfries," 128-29; "An Eclogue," 59, 61-64, 73, 78, 96, 99, 132; "An Eclogue to the Memory of Dr. William Wilkie, late Professor of Natural Philosophy in The University of St. Andrews," 59-61, 64, 78, 153; "The Election," 119-24, 151, 153-58; "Elegy on John Hogg," 124-128, 151; "Elegy on The Death of Mr. David Gregory," 19, 24-27, 32, 36, 117, 125; "Elegy on the Death of Scots Music," 36-40, 73, 77, 99, 104, 153-54; "An Expedition to Fife," 118; "The Farmer's Ingle," 89-96, 99, 111-12, 153, 160; "Fashion," 135; "The Ghaists: A Kirk-Yard Eclogue," 96-100, 111-12, 119, 132, 154; "Hallowfair," 64-70, 73, 83, 84, 120, 124, 153, 155-58, 160; "Hallowfair," 139-42; "Hame Content–A Satire," 103-6, 111-12, 132, 135, 154; "Horace, Ode 11, Lib. I," 23-24, 27, 32, 83; "The King's Birth-Day in Edinburgh," 40-45, 65, 73, 77, 84, 152; "The Lea-Rig," 139-142; "Leith Races," 106-11, 120, 124, 153, 155-56, 158, 160; "Ode to the Bee," 86-89, 100-101, 103, 105, 111, 113-15; "Ode to the Gowdspink," 87, 113-16; "On Seeing a Butterfly in the Street," 100-103, 111-15, 135; "Plainstanes and Causey," 78-83, 97, 111-12, 132, 135, 139, 153-55, 160; "R. Fergusson's Last Will" and its "Codicil," 30; "The Rising of The Session," 83-86, 111, 129-31, 154, 157; "The Sitting of the Session," 129-31, 154; "The Sow of Feeling," 29-30, 166n; "To Andrew Gray," 52-54, 111, 168n; "To My Auld Breeks," 135-39, 151, 155-57; "To The Principal and Professors of The University of St. Andrews, on their superb treat to Dr. Samuel Johnson," 116-19, 135, 151, 154, 157; "To the Tron-kirk Bell," 70-73, 78, 83, 153

Forbes, John, 20, 63
Forbes, Sir William, 142

Gay, John, 28, 149; "Trivia," 142-43
Gibb, Robin, 85, 130-31, 157
Girdwood, Geordie, 97
Gray, Andrew, verse letter to Fergusson, 52-53, 167n
Gray, Thomas, 22, 28, 159; "Elegy," 91
Green, Frederick C., 55, 167n
Gregory, David, 24-26
Greyfriars Churchyard, 97
Grosart, Alexander B., 97, 128, 165n, 166n, 167n

Hamilton of Bangour, William, 23, 100, 104, 165n; "The Braes of Yarrow," 104; "Horace, Epistle XVIII, Book I, Imitated," 100; "The Miss and the Butterfly, A Fable in the manner of the late Mr. Gay," 100
Hamilton of Gilbertfield, William, influence on Fergusson's "Elegy on Gregory," 25, 125; poetical correspondence with Ramsay, 50-52, 155, 167n
Henderson, Thomas F., 124, 165n
Henley, William E., 124, 165n
Henryson, Robert, 16; "Fables," 17; "Robin and Makyne," 61; "The Testament of Cresseid," 16
Herd, David, *Ancient and Modern Scottish Songs,* 140
Heriot, George, 97-99
Herriot, *see* Heriot
Hogg, John, 124-28
Holyrood, 143
Horace, 129

Irving, David, 89, 140, 169n

J. S., "To Mr. Robert Fergusson," 50, 73
James I, King of Scotland, 16-17; "The Kingis Quair," 16
Johnson, James, *Scots Musical Museum,* 139-40
Johnson, Samuel, 116-19

Kennedy, Walter, 70
Kinsley, James, 167n

Lindsay, Sir David, 70

Mackenzie, Sir George, 99
Mackenzie, Henry, 29-30, 166n
MacLaine, Allan H., articles by, 166n, 167n, 169n
Maitland, Sir Richard, 17
Martin, Burns, 165n
McDiarmid, Matthew P., 165n, 166n, 167n, 169n
Meyerfeld, Max, 169n
Milton, John, "L'Allegro," "Il Penseroso," 86; *Paradise Lost,* 92; *Samson Agonistes,* 114
Mons Meg, 42, 45, 167n
Montgomerie, Alexander, 16-17, 70; "The Cherrie and the Slae," 16-17
Mortmain Bill, 97-99
Morton, Richard, 167n
"Muirland Willie," 141

Oliver, John W., 165n

"Peblis to The Play," 17, 65-66, 167n
Perth Magazine, The, 52, 74, 89, 167n, 168n
Peterkin, Alexander, 165n
Philips, John, "The Splendid Shilling," 46, 136, 167n
Pope, Alexander, 22, 28, 149, 159

Ramsay, Allan, 18, 134, 158; anthologies of vernacular poetry: *The Ever Green, The Tea-Table Miscellany,* 18, 167n; influence on Fergusson, 23-24, 25, 32, 36-37, 50-52, 59-61, 65, 87, 90, 104, 125, 153-54; *writings of:* "Elegy on John Cowper," 154; "Elegy on Maggy Johnstoun," 25; "Elegy on Patie Birnie," 32, 37, 104; *The Gentle Shepherd,* 90; "Ode to the Earl of Hartford," 36; poetical correspondence with William Hamilton of Gilbertfield, 50-52; "Richy and Sandy: On the Death of Mr. Addison," 59; "Robert, Richy, and Sandy: A Pastoral on the Death of Matthew Prior," 59; "Third Epistle to William Hamilton of Gilbertfield," 23-24
Ritter, Otto, 169n
Robertson, James Logie, 90, 167n
Ross, Alexander, 155
Roughead, William, 55, 167n, 168n
Ruddiman, Thomas (ed. *The Weekly Magazine*), 20
Ruddiman, Walter (ed. *The Weekly Magazine*), 20, 32, 168n; *Choice Collection,* 130

Salmon, Charles, 128
Scots Poetic tradition, history of, 16-19; Fergusson's influence on, 20, 61-65, 90, 152-54, 158-63; dualism in eighteenth century, 18, 22, 37, 79, 87
Scott, Alexander, 16; "Justing and Debait," 17, 65
Scott, Sir Walter, *The Heart of Midlothian,* 36, 126
Sempill of Beltrees, Francis, 140
Sempill of Beltrees, Robert, "The Life and Death of Habbie Simson," 17, 25-26, 36, 140, 166n
Shakespeare, William, 159; *Love's Labor's Lost,* 91
Shelley, Percy Bysshe, "To a Skylark," 115
Shenstone, William, 20, 22, 28-29, 90, 159; "Pastoral Ballad," 29; "Schoolmistress," 90
Sillar, David, "Elegy on G. B.," 37; "Whisky," 65, 75, 166n, 168n
Skinner, John, "Monymusk Christmas Ba'ing," 65, 167n; "Tullochgorum," 32
Speirs, John, 147, 168n
St. Andrews, University of, 19, 24-27, 59, 63, 116-19, 124-28, 162
St. Giles Cathedral, 144-45
Swift, Jonathan, 145, 149; "Description of a City Shower," 143; "Description of the Morning," 142

Thomas, M. G. Lloyd, 167n
Thomson, James, "Castle of Indolence," 90; *Seasons,* 86
Thomson, William, *Orpheus Caledonius,* 141

Virgil, *Bucolics,* 89

Walker, Hugh, 55, 167n
Watson, George, 97-99
Watson, James (ed.), *A Choice Collection of Comic and Serious Scots Poems, both Antient and Modern,* 18, 65, 166n, 167n, 169n
Weekly Magazine or Edinburgh Amusement, The (published by Walter and Thomas Ruddiman), 20, 100, *passim*
"Wife of Auchtermuchty," 61
Wilkie, William, 19, 59-61, 63; *The Epigoniad,* 59
Wilson, Lieutenant, 128
Wittig, Kurt, 37-39
Wordsworth, William, 49; "I Wandered Lonely as a Cloud," 115

Young, Edward, *Night Thoughts,* 86